The purpose of this study guide is to provide supplemental educational material. It is not intended as a substitute or replacement of THE STARLESS SEA.

Published by SuperSummary, www.supersummary.com

ISBN – 9798604617199

For more information or to learn about our complete library of study guides, please visit http://www.supersummary.com

Please submit any comments, corrections, or questions to: http://www.supersummary.com/support/

TABLE OF CONTENTS

Erin Morgenstern, best-selling author of *The Night Circus,* published *The Starless Sea* in 2019. This work of magical realism interweaves separate stories with shared plots, themes, and characters. The book addresses ideas such as the concept of story, its meaning, and the nature of beginnings and endings, along with fate, free will, and what it means to become part of a narrative. This guide references the Knopf Doubleday first edition.

Plot Summary

Zachary Ezra Rawlins, an Emerging Media graduate student at a university in Vermont, discovers a book named *Sweet Sorrows* in the library. He is startled to find a story from his childhood within its pages. The book was donated to his university four years before his story took place. Intrigued, he begins researching the book and its mysterious symbols.

Zachary stumbles across a photo of a woman who wears three necklaces, each with a charm depicting one of the three symbols. He attends a masquerade ball and dances with a woman dressed as Max from *Where the Wild Things Are*; this woman, Mirabel, is the same woman from the photo. He also meets a storyteller who spins a tale. After the story ends, Zachary finds a card in his pocket. He goes to the meeting place listed on the card and encounters the storyteller from the ball, who goes by the name Dorian. Dorian asks Zachary to take a book to The Collector's Club headquarters and exchange it for another book. When Zachary returns with the other book, Dorian says he will take him somewhere.

This somewhere is the Starless Sea, a fantastical realm beneath the Earth from which all stories spring. Some visitors take up residency and study stories to their heart's content. Others dedicate themselves as acolytes, guardians, or keepers. The Collector's Club, led by Allegra Cavallo, works to destroy all doors to the Starless Sea—a door like the one Zachary walked away from as a child. Allegra wants to prevent new story seekers from entering, so the current story cycle playing out in the Starless Sea will never reach its end.

Zachary escapes the Collector's Club and reunites with Dorian. Running for their lives, the two come upon another painted door. While Zachary makes it through to the Harbor of the Starless Sea, the Collector's Club takes Dorian prisoner, so Mirabel and Zachary work together to rescue Dorian and bring him to the Harbor. Zachary then undertakes a quest given to him by a mysterious book, which charges Zachary with finding a man lost in time. The romantic tension between Zachary and Dorian escalates but is disrupted by a cataclysmic earthquake. They soon learn that the damage to the Harbor was caused by Allegra, who returns to the Harbor and tries to kill Dorian. A fissure opens up in the floor, sending Dorian and Allegra down to the surface of the Starless Sea.

Stories within the Starless Sea take place in in simultaneous yet separate timestreams. They share settings and characters, with the circumstances of one story sometimes changing the physical reality of another. A core story of Time and Fate continues in the form of a love affair between Mirabel, who is both immortal and the current incarnation of Fate (and also the painter of the mysterious entry doors that Allegra has tried to destroy), and the Harbor's Keeper, who is the incarnation of Time. After Dorian and Mirabel disappear, the Keeper shows Zachary a detailed portrait of himself and Dorian, painted 20 years before by Allegra. Mirabel takes Zachary down to the Starless Sea's shore to find Dorian—and bring about "the end" that Allegra has tried to prevent.

After his fall into the fissure, Dorian is rescued by Eleanor, who captains a ship on the Starless Sea made of honey. On the boat, Dorian finds Allegra's dead body. Meanwhile, after being separated from Mirabel, Zachary faces attacks from owls and the darkness, only to be rescued by the man lost in time: Simon. A member of the Keating family who donated *Sweet Sorrows* to Zachary's university's library, Simon has fallen in love with Eleanor, who entered the Starless Sea through the door as a child. The two then conceived a child born out of time: Mirabel.

Simon's attempt at recording "the story" of the Starless Sea causes Zachary to challenge his preconceptions and his own place in the greater narrative. Able to speak to Dorian yet separated from him by space and time, Zachary gives Dorian a sword. Zachary then finds an ice sculpture of Mirabel who asks Zachary to tell her a story; this story is the fulfillment of Zachary's test to become a keeper. Separately, Dorian retrieves Fate's heart, which was removed after her murder, and fights his way to the sea, facing imposters who each take the form of Zachary. When the two finally meet, Dorian accidentally kills the real Zachary with the sword. Zachary finds himself in a strange afterlife within a doll universe that he has seen within the Harbor. The bees who live within it inform him that he is the key to ending and locking up the story. The bees fly away, and the Starless Sea rises, absorbing everything back into itself, including the archived story.

Dorian agonizes over Zachary's death. As he waits to drown, he is rescued again by Eleanor. As he stares at

Zachary's body, he realizes that he has Fate's heart in his possession and pushes it into Zachary's chest. Dorian's true love comes back to life, and he and Zachary are finally united. After Zachary's story concludes, another begins, this time with the entrance of Zachary's friend Kat into another Harbor of the Starless Sea.

Book 1: "Sweet Sorrows"

Chapter 1 Summary: "Once, very long ago…"

A pirate is held in a basement jail with nothing for company but silent, disinterested guards—one sleeps his shift away, the other reads—and a terrified girl who leaves him food. After a few days, a new girl arrives to deliver his provisions. She is not afraid of him and leaves him watered wine instead of water—"bold and coy and clever" (5). The two soon strike up a silent companionship, sharing their food and water without conversation. The night before his execution, he twirls the girl's hair between his fingers. "Tell me a story," she asks the pirate (3). He agrees.

Chapter 2 Summary: "There are three paths. This is one of them."

In a city beneath the earth, there is a temple devoted to stories. It is a place of pilgrimage to some; others devote themselves to one of three paths: acolyte, guardian, or keeper. One young woman chooses the path of acolyte. She spends a month in isolation in a soundproof room, a test run for the silence that comes with the lifelong vocation of acolyte. It is her last chance to use her voice, and those who use their voices more tend to have more success: "Those who scream and cry and wail, those who talk to themselves for hours […] are ready when the time comes to proceed with their initiation" (7).

After a month of singing, the aspiring acolyte is offered the traditional metal disk with a bee carved in relief. She gives up her name, the bee is branded into her chest, and her tongue is cut out and burned. Acolytes "take an unspoken

6

vow to no longer tell their own stories in reverence to the ones that came before and to the ones that shall follow" (9-10). When she officially becomes an acolyte, "the stories begin to come" (10).

Chapter 3 Summary: "To deceive the eye."

The son of a fortune teller takes his usual shortcut on the way to school. Instead of graffiti on the alley wall, he discovers a shockingly realistic painting of a door. It is so realistic that he is surprised to feel the brick beneath the paint when he touches it. On the door are three symbols in a vertical line: a bee, a key, a sword.

Although he recognizes the door's magical properties, he chooses to leave it. The next day, the boy returns but the door has been whitewashed over, just like the usual graffiti.

Chapter 4 Summary

There is an authorless, burgundy book in a university library in Vermont. It was donated upon the death of its previous owner. Zachary Ezra Rawlins, a New Media Studies student in his second year of his master's degree, checks this book, entitled *Sweet Sorrows,* out.

The first two stories seem unrelated; one is about a pirate, the next about an acolyte. The third story, however, is about him: Zachary is the son of a fortune teller. Zachary is confused as to how a book older than him could possibly recount the events of a day in his childhood, a day of which he had never spoken to anyone. He wonders if he is the only real person in the stories, or if the stories reflect other real events and characters. He is caught by the last two words of the story: "And so the son of the fortune teller does not find his way to the Starless Sea. Not yet" (13).

Carefully, he removes the book's barcode on the book and discovers three familiar symbols: a bee, a key, a sword. "He wonders how, exactly, he is supposed to continue a story he didn't know he was in" (23).

Chapter 5 Summary: "Invented life."

Inside a room at the Harbor of the Starless Sea, there is a semi-sentient dollhouse: "What is remarkable is what has evolved around it" (26). Nearly everyone who enters the room adds something to the dollhouse, resulting in an ever-expanding, doll universe.

Chapter 6 Summary

Zachary Ezra Rawlins has determined that only one of the stories was about him, but he also notices several pages missing from the book. The stories in the book appear nested: The pirate tells the story of the acolyte, who experiences the story of the boy.

Seeking a distraction from his anxious thoughts, he goes for a walk and runs into Kat, a fellow Emerging Media student who creates interactive games. She asks his help in moderating a class on "Innovative Storytelling." In the class, students discuss what gamers want in a story and what makes a story compelling.

Students argue that gamers want to make their own choices within the framework of an existing narrative. Defining a story's meaning is even more complex, as it is personal and therefore variable in nature. One of the students, who knits throughout the class, says the following: "Even if you don't make the choices along the way, you decide what it means to you [...] Stories are personal, you relate or you don't" (35-36).

After the class ends, Kat tells Zachary that a participant named Elena wants to talk to him. Elena introduces herself as the library aid who helped him check out *Sweet Sorrows*. She has investigated the book and, while she has no information on the author, the book was donated from a private collection when the collector died. She offers to provide a list of the other books donated from that collection and hands him a slip of paper: *"From the private collection of J.S. Keating, donated in 1993. A gift from the Keating Foundation"* (38).

Chapter 7 Summary: "There are three paths. This is one of them."

In addition to becoming an acolyte in the underground temple of story, one can become a guardian. Guardians are chosen, then unknowingly observed by judges for months or years before their first tests.

One such test is given to a boy in a library. A woman in a green scarf asks him to watch a book for her. He agrees, she leaves, and time passes. Eventually, the boy becomes worried that he will need to leave before she returns. A woman in a green scarf comes and takes the book, but she is not the same woman. Despite her protests, the boy insists that he is watching it for someone and she cannot have it. The original woman returns for the book, giving him candy in thanks. Initial tests like these evaluate the potential guardian's propensity for care, respect, and attention to detail.

After passing 12 initial tests, the person is told that they are being tested to become a guardian. If they are from the world above the Starless Sea, they are brought to the Harbor, where they study and are tested on psychological strength, willpower, improvisation, and imagination. After three years, they are given an egg and told to return with the same, unbroken egg in six months. If they return with their egg, they take it to an elder guardian. They hold the egg up for inspection, but the elder guardian folds their hand around it, forcing them to crush the egg. The egg becomes a golden powder, which leaves a permanent shimmer on the potential guardian's hand, offering an unspoken lesson on responsibility and fragility.

The potential guardian begins the initiation and is given a tour of the Harbor, much deeper than the residents or even acolytes receive. After walking the shores of the Starless Sea, the potential guardians are seated and asked if they would give their life for it. Those who answer "yes" are tattooed with a unique sword designed specifically for them. Those who answer "no" are killed.

Unlike acolytes, guardians do not have a uniform or set of robes to make them identifiable. Their assignments rotate, and though most stay in the Harbor, some go to the world above, unnoticed. "They understand that what it is to be a guardian is to be prepared to die, always. To be a guardian is to wear death on your chest" (43).

Chapter 8 Summary

Since the library is closed, Zachary Ezra Rawlins goes to the local bar with Kat and another friend named Lexi. They discuss site-specific theater, a storytelling experience in which different locations tell different pieces of a story. When Zachary asks how such a method assures that the audience members all receive the entire story, Lexi answers: "You can't guarantee it but if you provide enough to see hopefully they can piece it together themselves" (45). As they prepare to leave, Kat insists that a man had been watching Zachary but has since left.

The next day, Zachary goes to the library to get the other 12 books donated by the Keating Foundation. One of these books is Bulfinch's *The Age of the Fable, or Beauties of Mythology*, which is blue with gilded details. After poring over the first 11 books looking for some hint of what *Sweet Sorrows* is and who may have written it, he decides to take a break and get some coffee. When he returns, the blue book is gone, though Elena says that no one has checked it out.

Once home, Zachary Googles information on *Sweet Sorrows*. An image search for the cryptic symbols produces a black and white, candid photograph of a masked woman wearing a necklace with three chains and a charm on each one: a bee, a key, and a sword. The image is in a photo gallery titled "Algonquin Hotel Annual Literary Masquerade, 2014." Zachary realizes that the current year's event is in three days.

Chapter 9 Summary: "A knock upon the memory of a door."

A door to the Starless Sea lies in a forest, rotten and rusted, without its knob. The house around the door has long since disappeared. A small girl wanders through the forest. She lifts the knocker and lets it fall with a resounding thud.

The girl falls feet first through the crumbling earth. Still, she is not afraid, only curious when she lands. The doorknocker is broken, the door is destroyed, and she is in the Starless Sea.

Chapter 10 Summary

Zachary Ezra Rawlins heads to New York City, to the Algonquin Hotel Annual Literary Masquerade. He considers why he has become so fixated on the book and its origins. He also considers that perhaps his story was a cautionary tale about missed opportunities, but the last words of his story—*"not yet"*—keep him searching for answers. He wonders why he believes that the story is real and where he should "draw mental lines, where to stop suspending his disbelief" (59). Ultimately, Zachary decides that, if nothing else, he knows he believes in books.

Chapter 11 Summary: "Those who seek and those who find."

There are many doors in varied locations, differing in style and condition, some well used and some never used. Each leads to the Starless Sea, drawing in story-lovers to visit it. Whether it is a book, a conversation, or a comfortable chair, everyone finds something they seek if they go through the door. Some even choose to stay forever, spending their lives at the Harbor of the Starless Sea, unconcerned about its future.

Chapter 12 Summary

Zachary Ezra Rawlins attends the masquerade ball, where attendees wear elegant costumes and offer strange methods of storytelling, whether in personal storytelling rooms or in the manner of the woman who hands out short stories she types on a typewriter. He dances with a woman dressed as Max from *Where the Wild Things Are*, but she soon leaves.

Someone—a man who is taller than him and smells wonderful—pulls Zachary through a doorway into pitch blackness. The mysterious stranger tells a story while guiding Zachary through darkened rooms and hallways. In the story, Time falls in love with Fate. Since this complicates fortune, which can be affected by both Fate and Chance, the stars worry what will happen if this love affair ends badly. The stars separate the lovers, but they eventually find one another again. Then, the stars ask the Moon what to do, and the Moon asks the parliament of owls.

After long consideration, the owls decide that if the issue is the combination or Time and Fate, the least important element should be removed. The owls rip Fate to pieces. No one interferes with the murder except a mouse who takes Fate's heart and safeguards it. The owl who ate Fate's eyes becomes the Owl King and has greater eyesight than any other creature.

Time continues, and the things that once were fated are now left to Chance, which never loves anything for too long—yet Fate finds ways to pull herself back together and impact events, thanks to the preserved heart, and "Time is always waiting" (73).

The storyteller guides Zachary to a new room. The door locks behind him, and he finds himself in a darkened corner of the hotel lobby. Unsure whether he has heard the vaguely familiar story before, he returns to the party and finds a card in his pocket. It says: *"Patience & Fortitude 1 a.m. Bring a flower."* (74). The back of the card has a bee on it.

Chapter 13 Summary: "There are three paths. This is one of them."

The third path, that of the keeper, is the oldest. The keepers have a different role than the other paths: "Devotion is for acolytes. Worthiness for guardians. Keepers […] are made keepers because they understand why we are here. Why it matters. Because they understand the stories" (78).

The keepers originally built the doors and the keys to go with them. Once, keepers kept only bees and their stories, but the role has changed over time. As with the other paths, a keeper's initiation involves training. The final training requires the potential keeper to pick any story that is not their own and study it for a full year. They study it not to learn by mere memory, but by heart "so that they can recall and relate the story as intimately as if they have lived it themselves and as objectively as if they have played every role within" (76).

After this year of study, the potential keeper is brought to a round room covered in keys—a copy of every key in the Harbor. In this room, the potential keeper tells their story. If they have passed the test, they are asked to pick one of the keys on the wall. The selected key is heated to brand the chest of the new keeper. After the branding, the keeper sees every door, every key, and everything kept within.

Chapter 14 Summary

Zachary Ezra Rawlins leaves to meet the mystery person near "Patience" and "Fortitude," who are the lions outside the New York Public Library. He grabs a paper flower from an arrangement on his way out but is knocked to the ground by a woman in a white fur coat; he dubs her the "polar-bear lady." He makes his way to the library early only to find *Sweet Sorrows* missing from his pocket.

The teller of the Time and Fate story appears with the missing book and introduces himself as Dorian. He says he's being followed by people who want to take the book. He warns Zachary not to let the people who are following him know that Zachary's story is in the book. When Zachary asks who they are, Dorian describes them as "a bunch of cranky bastards who think they're doing the right thing when *right* in this case is subjective" (83).

Dorian says that the plan is to go to the people's headquarters and have Zachary give them *The Age of Fable, or Beauties of Mythology*—the blue book which had gone missing from the library—in exchange for another book. He promises that if Zachary gets him the book, he will not only return *Sweet Sorrows* but also take him *there*. He announces that Zachary will not be able to get *there* without his help unless he has "an arrangement with Mirabel" (84).

Dorian gives Zachary a sword pendant on a chain and tells him to say he has a "drop-off for the archive" and that "Alex"—a code, not a person—sent him (85). Once inside, Zachary will be escorted to an unlocked room. When the escort leaves to answer the doorbell, Zachary will find a brown book in a case, swap the blue book for it, and leave through a back door.

Zachary wants to know who Dorian is, where he comes from, why Dorian cannot do the task himself, what is important about the book, who those people are, what the mouse did with Fate's heart, who Mirabel is, and when he can get his glasses back from the hotel. Dorian answers that they have a common destination and that he needs the book before he can go there. Dorian's voice is tinged with "storyteller cadence" again, prompting a flare of attraction in Zachary before he once again feels nervousness. Zachary finds the austere building and notices a plaque: *Collector's Club*. He rings the doorbell.

Chapter 15 Summary: "Lost cities of honey and bone."

A man is lost in time, searching for a woman he cannot remember. There are times when he remembers stories, but the stories he remembers combine with his memories, confusing him. He can no longer tell the difference between reality and fantasy. The bees once watched him, thinking that he was someone else: "They decided that one man out of his depth is no cause for alarm but even the bees are wrong from time to time" (90).

Chapter 16 Summary

Zachary Ezra Rawlins is finally answered at the Collector's Club door. A young woman says she will take the book, but he says that Alex sent him. She admits him. In the hall, countless doorknobs hang on ribbons, each with a tag. He tries to read them surreptitiously, catching city names, numbers—possibly coordinates and dates. She leads him to a door and unlocks it. As planned, the doorbell rings, and she leaves.

Zachary quickly finds the brown, leather-bound book in a case, as expected. The book reminds Zachary of *Sweet Sorrows* but is written in Arabic. He replaces the book with *The Age of Fable, or Beauties of Mythology*, and the case closes. On his way out of the building, he hears his escort on the phone. She announces that "he's here *now*" and that she thinks "he knows more than we expected" (96). She receives clear instructions of some kind, and Zachary realizes why she looks familiar: She is the student who was knitting in Kat's Innovative Storytelling class.

Zachary makes his way out of the building only to be stopped by the "polar-bear woman." She tells him that he is out of his depth and mistaken in whatever he believes is happening, and she offers to pay for his train back to Vermont and his ordinary life afterwards. Though Zachary is unsure whom he should trust—this woman and the student or Dorian—he swiftly escapes and finds Dorian, who ushers him into a cab.

Zachary tells Dorian about the woman in the coat and asks why Dorian stole the book. Dorian explains that it is his as much as anyone's. When Zachary asks if the people at the building are trying to get *there*, Dorian answers that they prefer no one uses that door anymore and implies that they destroyed Zachary's door, among others, by painting over it.

Now, Dorian and Zachary are on their way to a newly created door; like the others, it is painted by Mirabel—Max from *Where the Wild Things Are,* the costumed girl Zachary danced with at the party. They find the door, which has something written over it; Dorian says it reads, "Know Thyself." Zachary explains that it is the first half of the Rawlins family motto, the second half being "and Learn to Suffer" (101). Dorian suggests he try to change that part.

Zachary grasps the painted doorknob and opens the door but hears someone behind them. Dorian shoves him through as something wet splashes against him. Zachary expects to see blood but instead sees gold paint. Behind him, instead of the door, he sees only solid rock. He bangs on it, calling for Dorian, but there is no answer. Eventually, he walks down the stairs toward a source of light. At the bottom, he sees an elevator in the rock face, covered in patterns that include a bee, a key, and a sword aligned along its center seam. On the side, he sees a button. He presses it. The elevator opens.

Chapter 17: "...Time fell in love with Fate."

The pirate does not tell the girl only one story, but many stories nested within each other and connected to each other. After the story is over, she silently thanks him. She places her hand over her heart and bows, and he returns the gesture, signifying the end of their dance.

When he looks up, her hand is over the key on the wall. She unlocks the cell without waking the guard, and they walk up the stairs in silence. Just before they reach the door, knowing that they are doomed and will be found momentarily, the pirate kisses her: "But this is not where their story ends. This is only where it changes" (105).

Interlude I Summary: Another place, another time

In New Orleans, 14 years ago, a girl painstakingly paints a detailed door on a wall. She is startled by the fortune teller, who invites her for a cup of coffee. The girl agrees. The fortune teller serves the coffee, asks if the girl needs a place to stay, and offers her a set of tarot cards. She tells the girl that they are "cards with stories on them" (110), so the girl thanks the witch and takes the cards.

The fortune teller picks up the mug the girl had used and sees too much—"more people, more places, and more things than should fit in a single girl" (110). Madame Love Rawlins drops the mug onto the floor. She looks down the alley for the girl, but she is gone.

Book 1 Analysis

Book 1 introduces a nested narrative structure reminiscent of David Mitchell's *Cloud Atlas* and Mark Danielewski's *House of Leaves*: a series of stories that at first seem unconnected will come together as part of a larger narrative. After introducing Zachary, the book alternates between fairy tales and the continuation of Zachary's linear narrative. Zachary has already read *Sweet Sorrows* as he continues his story.

Emerging themes in Book 1 include the nature of story, the nature of reality, fate versus free will, and the determination of meaning. The nature of story—what it is and what it means—is most directly discussed in Chapter 4 during the class on Innovative Storytelling. Elena, the English literature student and occasional library assistant, describes the human desire for agency within a story—free will—which juxtaposed with a need for safety and structure: fate. Their interaction about story within video games illustrates a larger truth about story in the context of life: Humans want to feel they have some agency over their decisions, but many also long to be part of a larger plan and purpose.

The myth of Time and Fate, which will reappear in later chapters and become central to the narrative's climax, symbolizes the tension between fate and free will, as well as the question of how much control anyone has over the outcome of their own story. With Fate removed, only Chance determines what happens in Time, yet Fate sometimes finds a way to reassemble itself—the preserved heart, as will be revealed later, is part of that process. Characters in *Sweet Sorrows* are often unaware of the significance of a particular moment or the part it plays in their stories. Decisions made in these moments alter the trajectories of their stories, yet even when a character has accepted their place in a story, they may not know how to proceed, or they may have the wrong impression about where their story will take them.

Each story that isn't Zachary's introduces a character or setting that will be revisited in later chapters: the pirate and the girl who brings him food, the small girl who finds the door, the dolluniverse, the man searching for a woman but lost in time, the fortune teller who gives a girl some tarot cards. The boy who was tested as a guardian by the woman with the green scarf will later be revealed as one of the book's main characters. The girl who brought food to the pirate is also introduced in Book 1, although the connection between her current incarnation and who she was as the girl is not yet revealed. Madame Rawlins, the fortune teller, is Zachary's mother. The girl she gives tarot cards to is Mirabel—also Max from the masquerade ball.

Although Zachary's journey is one of wonder, it is also one of unanswered questions and peril. Mirabel is mentioned repeatedly as the painter of doors and as someone who has the power to take Zachary *there*. Dorian appears to be working with Mirabel, but what they're doing together remains unclear. Dorian, who asks Zachary to swipe the book from the Collector's Club—and to whom Zachary feels an almost instant attraction—disappears at the end of Chapter 15. As the novel continues, the Collector's Club will become more of an antagonist to Zachary, and the nature of its mission will be revealed. Already, the polar-bear woman and the knitting student actively work to dissuade Zachary from his quest.

The door that Zachary bypassed in his youth seems to be one of many doors that lead to *there*, a location called the Starless Sea. One girl goes through such a door in Chapter 9; although what's on the other side remains a mystery, she doesn't seem afraid of it. The nature of the Starless Sea is not entirely revealed, but the narrative mentions that it has a Harbor. Those who enter the doorways find what they're looking for on the other side and typically, never return. It is to this Harbor that Zachary heads in the next section.

As Zachary pursues the mystery of the book, he questions the nature of reality. *Sweet Sorrows* was donated to the library four years before Zachary found the painted door, yet his story is contained within. The story implies that, although he did not open the door and go to the Starless Sea that day, he eventually will. Zachary wonders what his place within this story (possibly within another story, nested in another) could mean for his life; as the knitting girl in Kat's class argues, reality's meaning is determined by the person who experiences it. In addition to wondering what's real and what isn't, Zachary wonders if he is also an agent within a larger story. Zachary has been chosen to test as a keeper, although no one has revealed this to him yet.

Book 2: "Fortunes and Fables"

Chapter 1 Summary: "The Star Merchant"

There is a merchant who sells stars in many forms: fallen, lost, and stardust, pieces in jewelry, items to display and gift, dust to use for magic. One night, he meets a traveler who asks what the merchant sells and is unimpressed at the answer, saying that he does not care for stars. The merchant laughs: "Everyone wishes to grasp that which exists out of reach. To hold the extraordinary in their hands and keep the remarkable in their pockets" (114).

The traveler answers by telling the merchant the story of Time falling in love with Fate. After the Owl King is crowned, the stars see Time's broken heart and wonder whether they did the right thing. They watch as the Owl King's mantle is passed through the generations, along with the Owl King's unnatural sight, which no mortal creature should possess. The stars "twinkle in their uncertainty, still" (115).

The traveler thanks the merchant for the wine and company, stating that same truth Dorian spoke: Fate will pull itself together, and Time always waits. In the morning, the merchant inquires whether the traveler has left. He is told that the tavern had no other guests than himself.

Chapter 2 Summary

The elevator takes Zachary Ezra Rawlins so far into the earth that he wonders whether it is really moving, but it eventually stops, opening into a lavish chamber with a curved, paneled ceiling. The door leading out of the chamber will not open. He finds a hidden alcove with a basin, and a black bag sitting in the basin. Inside the bag are dice and beneath the bag, in the basin, the word "roll" is carved. The dice have symbols instead of numbers: the familiar bee, key, and sword but also a crown, a heart, and a feather. He rolls the dice, each of the six landing on the same symbol: the heart. Immediately, the bottom of the basin falls out, and the dice and the bag disappear.

Zachary walks to the opposite wall and finds a matching alcove. Inside this one, he finds a glass with a tiny stem and a lid, and beneath it, the word "drink." The liquid is sweet and fragrant—with a lot of alcohol. Zachary is wracked with momentary dizziness, but recovers, his headache and grogginess gone. The door opens, and he enters the next room.

Zachary sees an architectural wonder resembling a cathedral. Through the wooden doorway, he finds "a cluster of glowing globes hung amongst brass hoops and bars" (120). The bars are stylized with golden hands at the ends pointing outward. The tiles above them are "laid out in a pattern of numbers and stars" (120). In the center of it all, a swaying pendulum hangs from the ceiling. He thinks it may be a model of the universe or a clock but is at a loss as to how to tell, let alone how to read it. Instead, he calls out, "hello." Someone answers him, asking whether he can be of assistance.

The man, who has a cat and who eyes Zachary's sword pendant, informs Zachary that the facility is closed and that he is not supposed to be there. Zachary says that he was helping a man who called himself Dorian and that he doesn't know "who the sword people are" (122), though he suspects they are guardians. The man wishes him good luck and escorts him the elevator, but pressing the button does nothing. The man asks if the door Zachary used was painted. When Zachary says yes, he mutters that he had "warned her that this would be problematic" and asks what Zachary rolled (122). Zachary answers truthfully—all hearts—causing the man to stare at him before directing him to follow.

The man says he knows that Zachary is there because he wishes "to sail the Starless Sea and breathe the haunted air" (123). He explains that they are in a Harbor, not the sea itself, and guides Zachary to his office, where a sword is displayed on the wall. The man asks about the location of the painted door. Zachary volunteers information about polar-bear lady, Dorian's possible danger, and the book he took on Dorian's behalf. As the man inspects the book, the Arabic text suddenly appears to be English. He thanks Zachary for bringing it back where it belongs, but says he may keep it for Dorian if he wants.

The man states that while someone certainly should rescue Dorian, Zachary will not be able to leave until Mirabel returns to escort him. In the meantime, he offers Zachary a room if he will give his name. The man identifies himself as "the Keeper." The Keeper hands Zachary "a round, gold locket on a long chain" with a bee on one side and a heart on the other (125). He also gives Zachary a compass which will lead him back to that spot—the "Heart." The Keeper guides Zachary to a room, gives him a key, and instructs him to ask if he needs anything.

Chapter 3 Summary: "The Key Collector"

There is a man who collects keys—old, new, lost, stolen, skeleton—but he is not greedy about them. He carries them in pockets and around chains, but gives them to those who ask, as he usually has a replacement key for whatever key they had broken or lost. For his kindness, people bring him keys from their travels, or they give him both spare and found keys as gifts. When his collection grows too large to wear, he displays them in his house. The house overflows with keys, which hang on the outside walls and the eaves of the roof.

One day, a woman knocks on his door, wearing a fine cloak with golden star-shaped flowers embroidered on it. She announces that she is hoping that one of his keys will unlock something that she seeks. After searching the house, she moves to the garden, finding a key hanging from a blooming tree. When the collector asks if the key will work for her lock, she answers that it is her key, which she lost long ago. She says she must repay him in some way, but he insists there is no need—he is glad to help reunite her with whatever locked-away thing she seeks. She corrects him: "It is not a thing. It is a place" (131).

The woman takes the key and holds it in front of her as if placing it into a keyhole, unlocking an invisible door in the garden. She opens it into a gilded room with high arched windows and countless candles. Beyond the door, music plays. The woman steps through the doorway, collects the key from the lock, and raises a hand to beckon the collector in. He follows, the door closes, and he is never seen again.

Chapter 4 Summary

Zachary Ezra Rawlins awakens and find himself in the Harbor. He sees more items than he remembers in his room, including a painting of a ship crewed by bunnies. He opens a wardrobe, which is full of handmade clothing in his preferred natural fibers. It all fits alarmingly well, down to the shoes. Despite his blurry vision due to his less-than-ideal contact lenses, he can clearly see the book he pulls from the shelves. He opens the brown leather book he stole from the Collector's Club. Thanks to the Keeper, the words are in English and each one is legible: *Fortunes and Fables*.

The breakfast the Kitchen provides is decadent. Zachary turns his attention to the book, a collection of fairy tales. He glances at a story of "a Girl and a Feather" before going back to the beginning, at which point a skeleton key falls out from the book's spine. Zachary wonders whether Dorian was seeking the book, the key, or both. The first story has another version of the story of Time falling in love with Fate. Zachary puts the skeleton key on the same chain as his room key and sends his clothes to be laundered. The Kitchen sends back the items he left in them: his wallet, his hotel key, and two scraps of paper, one from Dorian, the other ticket to the masquerade. With *Fortunes and Fables* in tow, he locks his room and ventures toward the Heart.

Zachary realizes that this place is not what he imagined after *Sweet Sorrows*: it's bigger. It feels infinite beyond what he can see, with a sense of "studiousness underlying a place of learning and stories and secrets" (139). The place has several cats, but he seems to be the only human besides the Keeper. He finds his way back to the universe clock. The Keeper confirms that Zachary is the only guest at present and offers him a selection of glasses. Mirabel has not returned, and mentioning this fact seems to make the Keeper unhappy.

As Zachary wanders down a different hallway, he notices several more paintings by the same artist as the painting of the bunny pirates. He wonders if he'll find the dollhouse mentioned in *Sweet Sorrows*, then sees a doll that looks like a woman with a calm expression on her face, eyes closed and smiling, "wrapped in a robe of stars" (141). Zachary continues his journey and finds a garden with a life-size statue of a woman sitting on a stone chair. Bees are tucked into every curl, crease of her gown, in her lap, and on her arms. By her feet, a glass is half-filled with wine, surrounded by bees.

Mirabel, now without the wig from her Max costume, has pink hair ranging from deep at the roots to pale at the tips of her shoulders. She informs Zachary that someone always leaves the statue a glass of wine around that time of year. She promptly informs Zachary that she knows exactly who he is, and they strike a deal that she will call him Ezra and he will call her Max. Mirabel is amused to learn that their mutual friend told Zachary to call him Dorian, observing that he must like him better as she was instructed to call him "Mr. Smith." Zachary informs Mirabel that Dorian never made it through the door and that the Collector's Club has him.

Chapter 5 Summary: "The Girl and the Feather"

There is a princess who refuses to marry a prince. Her
family disowns her and she leaves her kingdom, selling her
jewelry and hair to travel to a land far away. She asks an
old woman whether the land has a king only to learn that
the land is home to the Owl King. The princess becomes a
seamstress and marries a blacksmith, eventually telling him
the truth, but he thinks she is joking and playfully calls her
"Princess" from then on.

The princess gives birth to a daughter, a screaming baby
born on a night without the moon, an omen of bad luck.
Worried about the baby's future, she asks the old woman
what to do. The old woman tells her to take the baby to the
Owl King and have him see her future. They climb the
mountain to find the ruins of a castle. The princess tells her
daughter to wait and goes up the stairs. The girl sees a
golden feather. The ghosts are amazed by her ability to
wield the magical talisman. The girl tries to eat the feather,
then puts it in her pocket.

The Owl King demands to meet with the daughter alone,
and her mother agrees. Later, the princess is allowed back
inside, where only the girl sits in the light. The Owl King
speaks from the darkness, announcing that the child "has no
future" (148). The princess is displeased but unsure of what
she would have preferred to hear instead; she wishes that
she could go back in time and make different choices.

The Owl King asks the princess to bring the child back
when she is grown, and the princess agrees. The years pass,
allowing the princess to both forget and remember her
promise many times, sometimes questioning whether it
ever happened. The child has a mark between her waist and
her hip in the shape of a feather. The princess dies before

her daughter is grown, leaving her promise unfulfilled. The daughter soon disappears.

There are different versions of the next events: The girl either finds the castle empty, or she enters it but can no longer see the ghosts. In the rarest version, the girl finds her way back to find it lit and waiting for her. The Owl King acknowledges her return and they exchange greetings. The Owl King tells the girl to stay three nights in the castle. Then, she will have no desire to leave.

Chapter 6 Summary

Mirabel leads Zachary Ezra Rawlins back to the Heart, where the Keeper looks on. As they wait for the elevator, Mirabel explains that the dice and the drink were an "entrance exam," which she never took as she was born there. She offers him a candy from her cigarette case; the candy is a story. When asked if she knows the story, Mirabel answers that she does not, but she recognizes the patterns since all stories are about change. When he asks what "this" is, she answers that she will not have an answer that will satisfy him, but tells him that the secret to surviving after going down a rabbit hole is to be a rabbit.

Mirabel admits that she painted the door in the alley. She calls it a "litmus test" because if someone can believe enough to attempt to open a door which is painted, they will be more likely to believe in the place that it leads to, wherever that may be. The elevator opens "in between"— not in New York, and not *there*. It is an extension of the elevator, "like a tesseract except for space instead of time" (155).

After Mirabel takes him through a door, they open another incognito door into the Strand. They make their way outside and into a Starbucks at Mirabel's insistence. The normalcy jars Zachary. Mirabel orders "a grande honey stardust, no whip" (157). When asked, she tells Zachary she has ordered information. The drink is an Earl Grey tea with soy milk, honey, and vanilla, but it comes with six digits written on the bottom of the cup: 721909.

Zachary asks how Mirabel knows Dorian. She answers that Dorian once tried to kill her. Before he can ask more questions, they've arrived at the Collector's Club, and Mirabel inputs the numbers into the alarm's keypad. Looking at the doorknobs, Mirabel says that most of the doors were "lost before they were closed" (159). Now, *they* are tying up loose ends. She says that there are boxes of the less decorative knobs—all that is left after the doors are burned. They climb up the stairs to see a shadow in the hallway on the second floor. Dorian's body hangs from the ceiling just like the doorknobs, "tied and tangled in a net of pale ribbons" (160).

Chapter 7 Summary: "The Inn at the Edge of the World"

A widowed innkeeper's inn lies at a "particularly inhospitable crossroads" (161). While his inn was busy in the summer, he is in the depths of a long, harsh winter. One night, he falls asleep in his chair by the fire only to be awoken by a knock at the door. He opens it, letting in a woman.

The next morning, the traveler explains that she is supposed to meet someone there. The innkeeper warns her that there are no other travelers, but agrees to let her stay, insisting on no payment. They talk by the fire, and the wind listens as the innkeeper's world shrinks to the size of this inn—and the woman inside.

The next day, the traveler teaches the innkeeper how to make crescent-shaped buns. The innkeeper tells the story of how the wind travels up and down, searching for something it lost and howling its grief. In some of the stories, it is a lake; in others, a person whom it loved. In that case, the wind howls "because a mortal cannot love the wind the way the wind loves it in return" (166). The innkeeper asks if the traveler has any stories from her homeland. The traveler tells the story about when the moon and sun are missing from the sky. Every so often—100 years, 500 years, 1,000 years—the sun and the moon disappear at the same time. They coordinate their departure and meet in a secret location to discuss the world and compare what they have seen during that time. They meet, talk, and part until their next meeting.

The traveler for whom the woman is waiting arrives, dark in complexion, with light eyes and golden hair. The two talk for some time. Eventually, the innkeeper falls asleep. He wakes to the sound of the second traveler rising from her chair. The first traveler announces she has to leave in the morning. The innkeeper kisses her hand and asks her to "stay with" him and "be with" him. The traveler takes the innkeeper into her room and her bed as "the wind howled around the inn, crying for love found and mourning for love lost. For no mortal can love the moon. Not for long" (169).

Chapter 8 Summary

Zachary Ezra Rawlins awakes with an aching head, tied to a chair. A voice greets him from a speaker. The knitting girl from the Innovative Storytelling class brings in a tray with a teapot, not even looking at him. The polar-bear lady enters the room, her white suit and different-colored eyes reminding him of David Bowie. She introduces herself as

Allegra Cavallo. After confirming that Zachary is right-handed, she cuts the bonds on his left hand. She warns him that if he tries to untie his hand or escape, he will lose his left. He drinks the tea she gives him.

Allegra says that Zachary has already decided that she is the villain given his "superior meet-cutes" with Dorian and Mirabel. She tells him about her charity, which threw the masquerade ball, and discusses her other charitable works. Zachary is unconvinced, arguing that she is closing "one library to open others" (173). Allegra sternly informs him that the place is not a library. When told that she destroys doors, she retorts that she protects things—that she is protecting *there* from the world that is "too much" for it. She circles back to the stolen book, mentioning the tests of the guardians and implying that Dorian is causing a fuss over not being given the first book he ever protected. Recognizing the test from its description in *Sweet Sorrows*, Zachary says "you're guardians," surprising Allegra.

Allegra places an egg on the table, says the guardians protect the egg from breaking, and alludes to a changing order of things, from the guardians to her own system. She demands to know the location of *Sweet Sorrows*. She threatens Zachary (who thinks that Dorian had the book last), telling him that if he does not give her every detail he can remember about the book, leave Manhattan forever, and speak to no one about recent events, she will have her operative kill Zachary's mother. To prove her point, Allegra shows him a picture of his mother's farmhouse.

Zachary looks at the egg and informs Allegra that the egg is filled with gold. Just as Allegra asks what he said, the lights go out.

Chapter 9 Summary: "The Three Swords"

A sword maker makes an unexpectedly fine sword. As it is not commissioned, he is unsure of what to do with it. He takes it to the local seer to see the sword's future. The seer informs the sword maker that the sword will kill the king. The sword maker does not want to be responsible for creating the means of regicide, but neither can he destroy such a fine blade. Instead, he decides to make two more identical swords. Even he is unable to tell them apart: to tell which one will kill the king. He gives one sword to each of his three children, convinced that none of them will kill the king, "and if any of the swords fell into other hands the matter was left to fate and time and Fate and Time can kill as many kings as they please, and will eventually kill them all" (Page 179).

The youngest son takes his sword on his adventures, rarely taking it out of its scabbard. He falls in love with a man and has the sword melted down and turned into rings. He gives a ring to his love each year they are together. The man receives many rings.

The eldest son stays home and uses the sword for dueling. His skill earns him money, which he uses to sail. One day, he practices his swordsmanship on the deck. A sailor disarms him by the rail and the sword falls into the ocean, where it still sits.

The middle child, a daughter, keeps her sword in her library. She claims that it is only there as a decorative homage to her late father, but at night, she practices with it. She knows every inch of the sword, which is like an extension of her arm, appearing in her hand even in her dreams. One night, she dreams it is in her hand as she walks through a forest. She feels she is being watched, but sees no one. She finds a stump with books on top of it, and on top of the stack of books, a beehive with honey but no bees. Atop the beehive, there is a large owl, white and brown and wearing a crown. The Owl King surprises the girl by stating that she has come to kill him. He says that "they" always find a way to find him and kill him, even in dreams. She asks who finds and kills him, but he does not answer. Instead, the Owl King says: "A new king will come to take my place. Go ahead. It is your purpose" (Page 181). Though she has no wish to kill the Owl King, it seems like she is supposed to, so she beheads the owl in one stroke. His crown falls by her feet, but when she tries to touch it, it disintegrates into golden dust. When she wakes, a white and brown owl perches on the empty case where the sword once was. The owl stays with her for the rest of her life.

Chapter 10 Summary

Mirabel rescues Zachary and guides him to a room where Dorian's unconscious but living body is slumped. The relief Zachary feels is annoying; it implies an attachment to Dorian.

Mirabel locates a door, and they work together to drag Dorian to it. As they pull him along the corridor, Zachary sees a painting and recognizes the setting as the Harbor. As they make it to the elevator, Mirabel asks if Zachary trusts her. He answers that he does. Mirabel says, "someday I'm going to remind you that you said that" and produces a small handgun (185). She shoots the lantern on top of the cardboard on the other side of the doorway. The cardboard, wallpaper, and paintings all catch fire as the elevator doors close.

Chapter 11 Summary: "The Story Sculptor"

There is a sculptor who sculpts stories out of all kinds of things: snow, smoke, clouds, the space between raindrops. Her stories are fleeting due to the media chosen and too short-lived to be critiqued or questioned. Because people want her to sculpt using more permanent media, she begins to sculpt using materials like wax, arranged limbs of participants, knits, honeycombs. As she works with sturdier media, she discovers that she does not mind that her stories linger or that some enjoy them and some do not, because that is the nature of a story. Eventually, when she is much older, she agrees to work with stone.

After one show, a nervous, mouse-like man stays to speak with her. He tells her people are searching for something he has concealed and asks if she will hide it in a story for him. After three nights, the sculptor agrees to the man's request but asks not to know what he hides. She says that she will provide a box for it. For a full year, she works on nothing else, producing something unlike anything else:

> She created not one story but many. Stories within stories. Puzzles and wrong turns and false endings, in stone and in wax and in smoke. She crafted locks and destroyed their keys. She wove narratives of what would happen, what might happen, what had already happened, and what could never happen and blurred them all together (189).

A year later, the mouse-man returns. He places a mysterious, precious object in the ornate box the sculptor has created. She shuts the box, remaining the only one who knows how to close or open it. He kisses her lips as payment. She considers it fair. The sculptor does not hear from the man again, but many years later, those who seek what he has concealed find her. When they learn what she has done, they cut off her hands.

Interlude II Summary: "Another place, another time"

The pirate and the girl stand by the shore of the Starless Sea. The pirate imagines the life they could have had together if they made it onto a ship. He imagines it clearly, himself, free, "bound to nothing but her" (190). They pretend they have time as the alarm bells sound behind them, knowing that though death is imminent, their stories have much farther left to go.

They are found. The pirate screams as the girl faces her death, but she is not afraid: "She can see the oceans of time that rest between this point and their freedom, clear and wide. And she sees a way to cross them" (191).

Book 2 Analysis

The novel continues to follow the nested structure it has used thus far; new stories are introduced, and old ones are continued. A traveler who sells stars stops at an inn, where he hears the tale of Time and Fate, which was first told in Chapter 12 by Dorian at the masquerade ball. A man who collects keys reconnects a woman with a key she has lost; she unlocks a mysterious door and beckons him through, most likely to the Starless Sea—neither are heard from again. A princess who fled an arranged marriage arrives in a new town, marries a blacksmith, and has a baby. She takes the baby to the Owl King (descended from the original Owl King who ate Fate's eyes and thus gained extraordinary sight), believing the baby to be bad luck. The moon meets the sun at an inn and falls in love with the innkeeper. A sword is prophesied to kill a king. A sculptor of stories creates a box for Fate's heart, per the request of a mouse-like man.

In Zachary's continuing story, he arrives at the Harbor and meets a man who calls himself the Keeper. According to Book 1, Chapter 13, keeper is one of three paths (the others are acolyte and guardian); the Keeper currently in the Harbor notes Zachary's sword pendant, which indicates that Zachary is testing as a keeper. A new location in the underground world is revealed: the Heart, which houses a universe clock that changes in appearance from time to time. The Keeper gives Zachary a compass that will always guide him back to the Heart. He also connects Zachary with the Kitchen, which prepares wonderful food, and which will help Zachary in unexpected ways later. The Keeper himself shares an identity with one of the fairy-tale characters introduced earlier.

Above the majestic world below ground, the mysterious conflict between Mirabel and Dorian and the Collector's Club begins to take shape. Allegra Cavallo, the polar-bear woman, is the Collector's Club's ruthless head, determined to keep others from traveling to the Starless Sea through violent and even permanent means. Like many villains before her, Allegra believes herself to be a hero, valiantly protecting the Starless Sea; what she defends it from remains unclear. Allegra tries to persuade Zachary to her line of thinking, but fails to do so. Her decision to threaten Zachary's mother's life seals his conclusion that he must trust Dorian and Mirabel.

Mirabel seems to be working in opposition to Allegra, painting new doors even as Allegra burns them down. Mysteriously, Dorian has left the Collector's Club, of which he was once a member, yet he is also Mirabel's attempted murderer. Allegra also reveals that she and

Dorian are guardians (or related to guardians) and that Dorian is frustrated at not being in the first story he was given to guard.

The tale of Time and Fate appears again in this section, one of several tales about star-crossed lovers who cannot be together. Each pair—Time and Fate, the moon and the innkeeper, and the pirate and the girl—are separated by powers beyond their control, but each also hopes for a reunion. Zachary notes his continuing attachment to Dorian; although they are not yet a couple, they will experience this same separation—and hope for reunification—in later chapters.

Book 3: "The Ballad of Simon and Eleanor"

Chapter 1 Summary: "the naming of things, part I"

The girl who knocked on the dilapidated door in Book 1, Chapter 9 appears in a new world, still hanging onto the broken doorknocker. She only gives up the doorknocker when offered a stuffed bunny. She rarely speaks; no one can determine where she is from, and with her door broken, it would be difficult to send her back. They name her Eleanor, a fact that the painter tells the Keeper when asked. He repeats it, emphasizing the syllables at the end, but the painter does not ask about it, assuming the name has meaning to him.

No one takes charge of the girl they call Eleanor, as each assumes someone else will do it. She goes largely unnoticed as everyone else is busy with their own lives.

Chapter 2 Summary

Mirabel and Zachary take Dorian back to the Heart, discussing recent events along the way. Zachary is concerned for his mother, but Mirabel assures him that Allegra will only have Madame Rollins killed if she feels she has no other choice. Mirabel reminds him that Allegra had her chances to kill all of them but has not done so. Mirabel says that she hires people to do the work for her, nudging Dorian as an example. Mirabel asks for Zachary's story, which he gives her. She asks where *Sweet Sorrows* is now, and Zachary answers that he thought Dorian had it until Allegra asked where it was.

They arrive at the Heart. Since Dorian has never been there, he has to take the "entrance exam." Since he is unconscious, Mirabel and Zachary serve as his proxies. Mirabel warns Zachary to focus on Dorian and to concentrate on how Dorian would roll the dice; Zachary rolls one of each symbol, a flush. Mirabel drinks from the "drink me" glass because Dorian would. When they enter the Heart, Zachary hears Mirabel and the Keeper argue before the Keeper inspects Dorian and, although wary of the proxy exam results, lets them in anyway.

They take Dorian to Zachary's room, and Zachary notices that the paper flower in Dorian's lapel (the one Zachary brought to their initial meeting at the library, which he took from an arrangement at the hotel), which contained Italian text, has now been translated into English. After settling Dorian in, Zachary's world spins. Mirabel asks if he drank anything at the Collector's Club. He falls to the floor before he can answer.

Chapter 3 Summary: "a girl is not a rabbit, a rabbit is not a girl"

Eleanor sneaks around the Harbor, wearing a Venetian bunny mask and exploring rooms she is not allowed to enter. She writes her nightmares down, then makes paper stars out of them, leaving her fears about for the cats to play with. She does the same with pages she does not like in books. Once she lets the nightmares go, they are just another thing she does not remember, like the time before the Harbor.

In her explorations, Bunny Eleanor—who is different from the regular Eleanor who forgets things—goes places she is not supposed to go and opens doors she is not supposed to open. Bunny Eleanor finds a "burned place" hidden in the Harbor. Large bookshelves block it, but she crawls under them. Inside, she sees burned books, soot, what may have been a cat, and a door with a brass feather set into its middle. No matter what Bunny Eleanor does, the door does not open. She tries talking through the keyhole, but no one answers. Eventually, she writes a small note, signs it with a bunny face, and pushes it under the door. Nothing happens, so Eleanor leaves. While she is in another room, the door opens, pauses, then closes.

Chapter 4 Summary

When Zachary Ezra Rawlins wakes up, Mirabel berates him for drinking Allegra's tea The Kitchen has sent them incense, the strongest antidote it has. As the incense burns, an acolyte named Rhyme appears, silently asking what has happened. Mirabel gives a glib, one-sentence summary and introduces her to Zachary. Remembering a scene in *Sweet Sorrows*, he raises two fingers to his lips. Before he can feel too embarrassed at his presumption, Rhyme looks delighted and gives him a hand-over-heart bow. Mirabel leaves with Rhyme and instructs him to light another incense if it goes out before Dorian wakes up.

Curious, Zachary searches Dorian's chest for a sword tattoo. He doesn't find one, which prompts him to wonder how much in *Sweet Sorrows* was accurate. He does notice a tattoo of some kind on his back and neck, but all Zachary can see are "branch-like shapes." He returns to his chair to read *Fortunes and Fables*. He reads part of the story about the innkeeper and the traveler, then muses that at least Dorian has *his* book, even if he does not have his own. Then, Zachary hears Dorian's voice and is startled; Dorian says he put *Sweet Sorrows* in Zachary's coat.

Chapter 5 Summary: "time-crossed is not the same as star-crossed"

Simon lives with his uncle and aunt, though they do not treat him as a son and only mention his mother when they have something to blame her for. When Simon turns 18, he receives an envelope with a wax seal in the shape of an owl. Inside the envelope, there is a key, an address, and a note: "memorize & burn" (215).

Simon takes the key and goes to the address, where he finds a stone cottage in disrepair. Inside a book, he finds his mother's name: Jocelyn Simone Keating. When he opens the back door, it reveals a spiraling stone staircase. He follows the light down the stairs to an elevator and enters it; it opens to reveal a room with two pedestals and a large door. The pedestals have instructions. He drinks the contents of a glass and rolls the dice on the other pedestal: all crowns. The door opens, and he is greeted by an older man with white hair. The Keeper asks which door Simon used and confirms he is the son of Jocelyn Keating. The

Keeper frowns at the report of the dice and notes it in the ledger. He hands Simon a locket which will direct him to the entrance. The Keeper says that "initial visits are best kept short" (218), but Simon is welcome back any time.

Simon explores, eventually finding a door with the brass emblem of a heart on fire, partially blocked by a wardrobe full of books. It opens, prompting a black cat to exit the room. Inside, Simon sees five other doors, marked with different symbols. Across from the heart door he entered through, there is another; then, the five other doors have, respectively, a key, a crown, a sword, a bee, and a feather on their fronts. Above each door is a lamp, though the one above the key is out and the one above the feather is dim. A piece of paper slides out from under the feather door. The note reads, "Hello. Is there someone behind this door or are you a cat?" (220) A rabbit is drawn beneath the text.

He unlatches the feather door, opens it, and finds no one there. He writes, "I am not a cat" on the back of the note (221), then slides it under the door. He opens the door again, and the note is gone. Then, the door opens suddenly, revealing a woman with bunny ears. She says her name is Lenore and she came from the "burned place." Simon confirms that he wrote the note, but while he wrote it only moments before, she wrote hers—and delivered it—eight years before. As she inspects the door, Simon realizes that Lenore is quite pretty with her dark skin, darker eyes, and pretty, braided curls. She asks if there are bees "in here," but he says there are not.

When asked, Simon tells Lenore about his cottage and its door. They eat Lenore's honey as they talk, sharing information and secrets, and his attraction to the strange girl intensifies. She wants to show him her favorite book, so she pulls him along through a door. When she steps out of one room and into another, she disappears along with the room. He is in the burned place that she mentioned, and she is gone. After a few minutes, she reappears in different clothing with a gilded book. To Simon's surprise, she informs him that it has been six months since she has seen him and she has regularly opened the door to find the space he stands in empty. Simon says that it is impossible and goes to prove it by stepping back into the hall. When he turns, Lenore is gone. He is left with only the book as proof that he did not imagine her.

Chapter 6 Summary

Zachary Ezra Rawlins finds *Sweet Sorrows* in his coat pocket, just as Dorian said. Relieved, he thumbs through it, finding more missing pages than expected. Zachary explores the Harbor again; in one room, he finds a fountain with coins in it and an entryway to a dimly lit hall, which is blocked by an armchair and a bookshelf. The hall has closed doors with no doorknobs or handles, only locks. One of the door has charring along its jambs. He sees something move at the end of the hall, but when he looks up, he sees nothing.

Zachary returns to the fountain, considering his prolonged and arguably growing attraction to Dorian and finding it annoying. He passes by a painting of a candle only to notice it is not a painting, but a frame hung around an actual, burning candle. When he blows it out, the frame lowers, showing an opening in the wall. He climbs through and finds himself in the room with the dollhouse, which he'd read about in *Sweet Sorrows*, but the whole room is burned. He finds a single, porcelain, female doll, unbroken but cracked. Zachary realizes that he wanted to see the doll universe as *Sweet Sorrows* had described it. He notices a few other surviving pieces: a shipwreck, a grandfather clock, and a deer.

Zachary finds his way to the Heart and asks the Keeper what caused the fire. The Keeper responds, "An accumulation of unforeseen circumstances, an accident" (233). Zachary confirms that the Keeper, Rhyme, Mirabel, Dorian, and himself are the only current residents of the Harbor. The Keeper informs him that the others have left, died, returned to their original places, or left to find new ones. When asked, the Keeper says that he stays because it is his job and calling. He asks why Zachary is there. Zachary repeats what the Keeper said before, that he is there "to sail the Starless Sea and breathe the haunted air" (234).

Zachary asks if the Harbor ever housed anyone named Keating, causing an unreadable expression on the Keeper's face. The Keeper answers that several people who held that name visited long ago. Zachary decides not to show *Sweet Sorrows* to the Keeper and returns to his room to find a note slipped under his door. He wonders if the lines are a puzzle or part of a poem or story: "The Queen of the Bees has been waiting for you/Tales hidden within to be told/Bring her a key that has never been forged/and another made only of gold" (235).

Chapter 7 Summary: "book borrowing"

Simon is tired, hungry, and confused by his situation. He returns to the Heart and tries to open the door, but it will not budge. The Keeper informs him that he cannot take the book with him without leaving something in its place. He offers the broom he had brought with him from the cottage. When he gives the Keeper the name of the book, *Sweet Sorrows*, the Keeper asks where he got it. Simon answers that Lenore had lent it—her favorite book—to him. The Keeper gives the book back.

Back in the cottage, Simon finds a trunk that belongs to his mother. Inside are documents, notes, and papers of stories, "long rambling things about reincarnation and keys and fate" (239), a letter from someone named Asim, and books and maps in various languages he cannot read, with a variety of notes and symbols: crowns, swords, and owls. Finding *Sweet Sorrows* again, Simon remembers that his journey isn't a dream. He returns to the Harbor and makes his way to the door with the heart on it. The feather door opens and he sees Lenore. They waste no time, kissing and stripping each other. Lenore keeps the bunny ears on. Their love is passionate but doomed.

Chapter 8 Summary

Zachary Ezra Rawlins finds the statue of the woman covered in bees. He wonders if she is the Bee Queen from the poem, and if so, how to give her keys. He walks down a new hall and finds something like a gumball machine, which dispenses copper balls filled with long, thin stories printed on something like ticker tape. Zachary receives a story about "lost loves and castles and crossed destinies" (241). He continues past a ballroom and finds Mirabel, who is reading *A Wrinkle in Time* to find out whether tesseracts affect space as well as time.

They share a drink, and Mirabel suggests that *Sweet Sorrows* might have come from the Archive, which only acolytes may enter. Zachary asks who wrote the book and why he is in it, but Mirabel answers that she has heard that "records kept in the Archive aren't exactly chronological" (245). Allegra, Mirabel explains, wants to keep all of it locked up to keep it safe from something—though she is uncertain whether that something is people, progress, or time.

Mirabel confirms she was the woman with the necklaces that Zachary saw in the photo—the photo that sent him in search of the literary masquerade ball. She lets Zachary borrow the golden key from her necklace. He asks where the Starless Sea is, and Mirabel takes him down a long, dark stairwell. The stairs end far above the sea; the champagne bottle Mirabel drops takes minutes to hit something. Mirabel explains that the sea receded. Zachary asks if that is what caused the exodus or if the exodus caused the receding of the sea. Mirabel answers that it could be neither or both, but she feels that time is the culprit: "The old doors were crumbling long before Allegra and company started tearing them down and displaying doorknobs like hunting trophies" (248).

Mirabel informs him that the "heyday" of the Starless Sea was over long before her birth, but Zachary protests that *Sweet Sorrows* suggests differently. Mirabel says the book is only an interpretation of reality: He wants the real place to be just like the book, but this is not possible because the words in a book don't encompass a place. The place lives in the imagination of the reader. Zachary asks if fixing the doors would make people come and restore the Starless Sea to its former state. Mirabel says that people come, but they do not stay. He returns through the ballroom and pirouettes, making Mirabel laugh.

Zachary follows Rhyme, watching her go through a door in a stone wall after pressing something metal into the bee design imprint. When she returns, she places a book on a table. It is small, gilded, and reminiscent of *Sweet Sorrows*. The text is handwritten, and the title is *The Ballad of Simon and Eleanor*.

Chapter 9 Summary: "a short lecture on the nature of time"

Simon and Eleanor spend as much time together as they can, but they eventually need food. Eleanor suggests that they try another door besides the feather door. The bee door will not open, the sword door has no knob, and the crown-door opens into a pile of stone and a collapsed hall. Eleanor picks the lock of the key door with her necklace. They entwine their fingers and step through it.

Immediately, Eleanor fades from Simon's grasp. He calls out for her, but she doesn't answer. He makes his way back to the heart door, but its doorknob is missing and its keyhole has been filled in. Simon goes back to the Heart and asks the Keeper to open the door, but he answers that access to the room beyond that door is forbidden.

Simon protests that he has gone through it before and met Lenore there. At the Keeper's direction, Simon describes his lover. The Keeper states that there is no such woman in residence and he must be confused. Simon insists that he is not. The Keeper finally tells Simon that there are places deeper than the Heart, where time is "less reliable." Simon resists the idea, insisting that the Keeper unlock the door. The Keeper answers that the door has not been locked but has been closed as a necessary precaution; it will not open for any key.

Despondent, Simon asks how he can find Lenore again. The Keeper answers that he must wait and that he understands the pain of separation. They argue, but Simon's frustration has no effect on the Keeper. The Keeper describes time as a river with inlets: Simon has stepped into an inlet, as has Lenore, albeit from a different time. Simon asks if there are other inlets, and the Keeper answers that it is not wise to think that way, suggesting that Simon go home as he will not find what he seeks. Simon takes a compass and continues walking away from the Heart, intent on going as deep as he can toward the Starless Sea, in search of the inlets where time may run differently.

Chapter 10 Summary

Zachary Ezra Rawlins reads the book Rhyme left for him until the words are jumbled again. He finds his hotel keycard and realizes that it is a key which has not been cast; along with Mirabel's golden key and his uncast hotel key, he now has both keys that Bee Queen requires. He knocks on Dorian's door only to find him very drunk and reciting the story of the three swords, where the girl kills the Owl King in her dreams. When he says that the owl remained with her for the rest of her life, he motions to the nearby painting of a white and brown owl with a crown above his head.

Dorian falls asleep, and Zachary walks to the Heart, where he overhears a conversation between the Keeper and Mirabel. The Keeper insists that something will not work, but Mirabel argues that he cannot be sure of it and that "he has the book" (259). The Keeper says that Mirabel should not have gotten Allegra involved, but Mirabel protests she was already involved since she began closing doors and, along with them, their associated possibilities. Mirabel insists that they needed "him" and "that," motioning to something Zachary cannot see, and reminds the Keeper that the book has been returned. She says that the Keeper has given up. He responds that he doesn't want to lose her again; Mirabel says that maybe this time will be different.

Zachary returns to the Bee Queen statue. In one hand, he places Mirabel's golden key; in the other, he lays the keycard. The sculpture moves, grasping the items and revealing a staircase beginning from the back of the chair. Seeing a light at the bottom of the stairs, Zachary steps down into the darkness.

Chapter 11 Summary: "the naming of things, part II"

Eleanor is overwhelmed with caring for her perpetually crying infant daughter and heartbroken over never seeing Simon again. Sometimes, the painter or the poets watch the baby for a few hours, but Eleanor has her the rest of the time. The Keeper, not helpful with the baby, informs Eleanor that she never sees Simon again. The Keeper knows this because Simon never saw Eleanor again—he was there to know, after all.

Eleanor sends the Kitchen notes asking for help and advice. The Kitchen sends up milk for the baby and suggests that she read to the baby to calm her. Eleanor misses *Sweet Sorrows* and regrets having torn out the pages she did not like as a child; they still litter the Harbor as stars. She tries to remember why she did not like those particular pages and remembers a few things: a sorrowful part about a stag in the snow, a rising sea, someone with a lost eye. She considers that she herself may be a page torn from a story, made into a star.

Eleanor remembers enough of *Sweet Sorrows* to recount some of it to her baby: the pirate and the girl, the dollhouse, and the unusually familiar story about the girl who knocked on a door and fell through it. That story seems so familiar she sometimes believes she may have lived it. The Kitchen sends up a stuffed brown bunny for the baby. Eleanor has never felt a sense of belonging there, but if she ever did, she feels it less now. She asks the Kitchen what to name the baby. It answers: Mirabel.

Interlude III Summary: "Another place, another time"

Two weeks earlier, Dorian sits in the local bar, nursing a scotch and ostensibly reading a book. He watches Zachary, Kat, and Lexi. He expected Zachary to be a collegiate cliché of a boy and a socially anxious hermit, but instead, he sees an intriguing young man. For some reason, Dorian finds that he cannot read him the way he can read everyone else: "A man he can't read. It is as vexing as having a book he cannot touch. An all too familiar frustration" (266).

He watches as a girl slips clear powder into the sidecar prepared for Zachary. Despite having done the same thing before when working for the Collector's Club, Dorian decides to stop it. He knocks into the waitress on her way to deliver the poisoned drink, ensuring that Zachary does not drink it. He wonders how everything had led to this: one book and one excessively interesting man. Kat catches Dorian staring at Zachary and he realizes he should not be here: "He should have walked away a year ago, after a different night in a different city when nothing went according to plan" (269). He could forget everything and run, but instead, he watches Zachary through the window and thinks, "Let me tell you a story" (269).

Book 3 Analysis

Book 3 reveals further connections between the fairy tale characters and those in Zachary's story. Simon Keating proves to be Mirabel's father and the man lost in time who is searching for his lover. Eleanor is the girl who knocked on the fallen door, the bunny girl who stole *Sweet Sorrows*, and Lenore, the woman who falls in love with Simon and gives birth to Mirabel. Just like Zachary, she reads about her own story in *Sweet Sorrows*.

Zachary explores places from Eleanor's story: a hall blocked by a bookshelf, with the series of doors that so vexed Eleanor and Simon, and the burned dolluniverse room. The effects of nonlinear time are evident in the way that Zachary's and Eleanor's stories interact. Zachary, for instance, notes more missing pages from *Sweet Sorrows* when he finds it again. In her own timeline, Eleanor has torn out stories she didn't like— a heartbreaking story about a stag, a rising sea, and someone with a lost eye, who will turn out to be Allegra—folding them into paper stars. The events from her timeline are interacting with the physical reality of Zachary's timeline.

Both within Zachary's story and in the fairy tales, characters explore the nature of time and reality. Mirabel reads about tesseracts from *A Wrinkle in Time,* which are fifth-dimension shortcuts through space and time. The Keeper also explains his view of time as nonlinear when he tries to help Simon understand why he can't find Eleanor. Time runs in one direction like a river, though inlets can be entered and connect to multiple points in the timestream.

Like clues left by others for the current inhabitants of the Harbor to follow, the themes and stories mentioned by various sources have elements that either appear in other stories or foreshadow events to come. Zachary's story from the gumball dispenser is about "lost loves," castles, and "crossed destinies." The observed symbols—a bee, a key, a sword, a crown, a heart, and a feather—are repeated on doors and on dice, though they are not fully explained. As the stories of star- and time-crossed lovers converge, Zachary discovers that Mirabel and the Keeper are also in love, having lost each other at least once. They join the other separated lovers: Simon and Eleanor, the moon and the innkeeper, Time and Fate. The attraction between Zachary and Dorian proves to be increasing, as is the likelihood that they'll be parted, either temporarily or forever.

Book 4: "Written in the Stars"

Chapter 1 Summary: "a paper star folded from a page removed from a book"

There is a stag standing in the snow amongst the trees, and he will vanish in the blink of an eye. He may be a stag, or he may represent something else: "The stag is a shot left untaken. An opportunity lost. Stolen like a kiss" (273). He may pause longer than he used to in these new times, which are more forgetful than they once were. Although it would have been unthinkable once, the stag waits now for someone to take the shot, piercing his heart. He waits "to know he is remembered" (273).

Chapter 2 Summary

A Persian cat follows Zachary Ezra Rawlins as he descends down the stairs that appeared behind the Bee Queen. When the cat executes a graceful move, Zachary calls it a "show-off." A voice repeats the word back. Zachary tells himself it is only an echo, but the cat hisses at the darkness. He continues on, finding a lamp and a key. At the end of the hall, he sees an alcove with a second lamp and an arched stone door with a keyhole. Zachary unlocks the door. The cat hisses into the darkness and runs away, but Zachary enters the crypt, where bodies lie wrapped in memories of each person's life before their death. He also sees an urn full of ashes.

Some of the columns in the crypt have indentations carved into them, which makes them look like podiums. One holds an ancient-looking, loosely bound book. Zachary picks the book up and it breaks into pieces. He is able to read a sentence from the fragments: "Hello/son/of the fortune-/teller" (277). He continues to find fragments with cryptic instructions: "There are three/things lost/in time [...] sword/book/man [...] find/man" (277). He considers the man lost in time in *Sweet Sorrows* and wonders how he is supposed to find, at the behest of ghosts discussed in old books, someone lost in time.

Zachary takes the key back from the door, which swings shut. He hangs the key back on its hook and returns the lamp to its shelf. He glances down the hallway to see a shadow in the shape of a human staring at him. As soon as he blinks, it disappears. Zachary runs back up the stairs as fast as he can.

Chapter 3 Summary: "a paper with a single bent corner"

An account of a nightmare, number 113: A girl cannot get out of a big chair. Her arms are tied to it, but she has no hands. She is surrounded by people without faces who feed her pieces of paper. On the paper are written "all the things [she] is supposed to be" (279). They never ask her what she is.

Chapter 4 Summary

Zachary Ezra Rawlins heads back to the elevator and ascends from the Harbor, attempting to go back to the life he had before all of this. He makes it halfway home before he realizes the door at the Collector's Club was burned down, and he has no way to return. He goes back to his room in the Harbor to find a blue sticky note on the center of his door, "All you need to know has been given to you" (280). He takes it inside, reading it over and over again, then puts it on the frame of the painting of the bunny pirates.

Zachary sends a note asking the Kitchen if "this" is real. The Kitchen answers in the affirmative and says they hope he feels better soon, sending along cupcakes and a warm drink. The next morning, he considers that he does not understand what time really is. The Kitchen sends up coffee and breakfast and says they hope he has slept well. Instead of the usual gratitude, he writes back, "I love you, Kitchen" (283). The Kitchen responds, "Thank you, Mr. Rawlins. We are quite fond of you as well" (283).

Zachary wonders where a man lost in time would be, then remembers that he supposedly has all he needs to know. He continues reading the book Rhyme gave him, *The Ballad of Simon and Eleanor*, but the text stops midway through the book, leaving nothing but blank pages. He wonders whether the stories in *Sweet Sorrows, Fortunes and Fables,* and *The Ballad of Simon and Eleanor* are all part of the same story. He also wonders how to find Simon, ponders the burned room and the broom now in the Keeper's office, and considers how the story ends for the son of the fortune teller.

Zachary picks up the origami star he collected before and notices writing on it. He unfolds it into a long strip of paper and sees that it describes another nightmare. Zachary returns to reading *The Ballad of Simon and Eleanor*, pausing at the final word in the book. He goes to find Mirabel.

Chapter 5 Summary: "combined contents of several paper stars (one has been partially chewed by a cat)"

On exceedingly rare occasions, acolytes choose to sacrifice something other than their tongues. The painter mistakenly believes that choosing the path of the acolyte will rekindle her love of this place, which has changed over time just like everything else. She expects to sacrifice both of her eyes instead of her tongue, but the acolytes only take one. Suddenly, her mind is flooded with images beyond her ability to paint and she realizes that "this path was not meant for her" (286), but it is too late.

Chapter 6 Summary

Zachary Ezra Rawlins sets off to find Mirabel. He collects a bottle of wine and finds another hidden room. Inside the hidden room, he notices several framed paintings, one of which draws his attention. It depicts a forest at night, with a crescent moon shining between branches; a massive birdcage sits in the forest, but on its perch, a man sits and faces away. Keys and stars litter the trees around the cage; they sit in nests and on the ground, and they hang from the branches on ribbons. The painting reminds Zachary of the bunny pirates, and he wonders if these paintings—and the bee lady—were all created by the same artist.

Dorian, standing barefoot, also observes the painting. He is surprised to see Zachary; he believed he was having a dream. Dorian rests his hand on Zachary's chest to feel his heartbeat and assure himself that they are both truly *there*. Zachary tells Dorian about his unsolved mysteries and his search for Mirabel. Dorian is skeptical about his new commission to find the man lost in time, but Zachary convinces him to read *Sweet Sorrows* and *The Ballad of Simon and Eleanor* before casting judgment.

The two discover that within the Harbor, both books and spoken language are translated for the reader/listener into whatever they can understand. As they read, Dorian informs Zachary that the story in *Sweet Sorrows,* about the boy watching a book for a woman in a green scarf, is about Dorian. Only the beginning applied to Dorian; he never underwent additional tests.

When Zachary calls him a guardian, Dorian corrects him, saying he was a member of the Collector's Club, which may have evolved out of the guardians. He goes on to explain that Allegra promised all the Club's members passage to the Harbor, but only after securing it properly through destroying the doors. He shares that he was a devout follower until one night—and becoming acquainted with Mirabel—made him run away. The Collector's Club responded by destroying his aliases, but he successfully disappeared into Manhattan.

Going back to his new mission, Zachary says that a book, a sword, and a man are lost in time. The book, *Sweet Sorrows,* has been returned, and the Keeper has a sword in his office—"all conspicuous"—so Zachary reasons that the man is the only one still missing. Dorian suggests that Simon is the man lost in time. Zachary mentions his bunny pirate painting—he believes the same painter created all the paintings in the Harbor—and Dorian asks to see it. On their way back to Zachary's room, Dorian looks through a telescope at a cracked ship that was once on the Starless Sea, books stacked on its deck.

Zachary asks why Dorian helped him in New York, and Dorian answers that he helped because he wanted to do so. After reaching Zachary's room, they look at the bunny pirate painting; Dorian thinks it was painted for Eleanor, who loved rabbits. They share the bottle of wine, and

Dorian thanks Zachary for rescuing him from the Collector's Club. Zachary is once again startled by the intimacy of his thoughts, feeling as though he has known Dorian forever. Zachary asks why people came to the Harbor of the Starless Sea. Dorian answers that, like them people come "in search of something [...] Something more. Something to wonder at. Someplace to belong. We're here to wander through other people's stories, searching for our own" (297).

Dorian then toasts "to Seeking," and Zachary responds "to Finding"—it's the expected response given in *Fortunes and Fables*. Dorian observes that it is nice to have someone read the stories which he knows "so intimately." Dorian asks Zachary's favorite and he responds that he likes the three swords story and the innkeeper's story, but he feels that so many of them are sad, leaving him wanting "more"—not necessarily a happier ending, but a more complete and satisfying resolution.

Dorian notices the wardrobe and asks whether Zachary has checked it for Narnia. Zachary is shocked that it had not occurred to him, and Dorian goes to have a look. As Zachary ponders Dorian's storytelling ability, which transcends the need for words—and how much he would like Dorian to touch him the way he is touching the sweaters—Dorian disappears into the wardrobe.

Chapter 7 Summary: "a paper star that has been so mangled by circumstance and time that its shape is only vaguely recognizable as a star"

The acolytes cannot predict when the man lost in time will find his way back in or out of it again. There are not as many acolytes as there once were, so when the man appears and knocks a candelabra over, they are not in the room to put out the fire. The fire blazes down the halls until it reaches the room with the dolls, which "it claims it for its own, an entire universe lost in flame. The dolls see only brightness and then nothing" (300).

Chapter 8 Summary

Zachary follows Dorian through the wardrobe into what seems to be a dark stone tunnel. They hold hands, ostensibly to keep from being separated in the dark. They find a room filled with doors that have unique images on them. One shows a girl holding a lantern up toward the sky, which is filled with angry birds that direct their fury at her; Zachary and Dorian agree not to open that door. The next door displays a city with curved tower, an island under the moon, and a figure in a cage reaching for another figure in another cage (it reminds Zachary of the pirate and the girl). He wants to open it, but Dorian directs him to another door: a celebration under a banner with the phases of the moon carved on it. They both enter but are separated.

Zachary finds himself in a hallway and meets a man with red hair. The sensation of touching his shoulder does not feel quite right; it's more the idea of touch than the actual feeling. The man sees him, and asks if he is there for the party, but refers to him as a ghost moments later to someone else. The book he was reading has poetry by Sappho: "someone will remember us/I say/even in another time" (303). He follows the music into another hall, then the tide of people into the ballroom. An acolyte has a bowl of gold paint, into which people dip their hands. Suddenly, someone presses a piece of paper into his palm. Written in gold is the beginning of a story:

The moon had never asked a boon of Death or Time but there was something that she wished, that she wanted, that she desired more than she had ever desired anything before. A place had become precious to her, and a person within it more so. The moon returned to this place as often as she could, in stolen moments of borrowed time. She had found an impossible love. She resolved a way to keep it (305).

Zachary cannot see Dorian, but he is sure that Dorian must have written the story and must be somewhere in the ballroom. A woman is dressed in ribbons with stories written on them. One ribbon catches his eye: "First the moon went to speak with Death" (306). He finds another continuing the story: "She asked if Death might spare a single soul. Death would have granted the moon any wish within her power for Death is nothing if not generous. This was a simple gift, easily given" (306). No other ribbons mention the moon or death, so Zachary walks away. He thinks he sees Dorian, so he continues in that direction, but the red-haired man from before catches him, asking him when he is. The man touches Zachary's face and, this time, he feels it properly. He moves to bring Zachary to the dance floor, but the crowd separates them.

Zachary finds a wall with more of the story on it. The moon asks Time to leave a space and a soul untouched. Time eventually agrees, only if the moon will help Time find a way to hold onto Fate. The moon agrees, though she does not know how to undo what has been done. "And so Time consented to keep a place hidden away, far from the stars. Now in this space the days and nights pass differently. Strangely, slowly. Languid and luscious" (307).

Still looking for Dorian, Zachary sees the Keeper, who is watching someone intently, but Zachary cannot tell who it is. Zachary sees the Starless Sea, full and resplendent. He steps toward it, but Dorian pulls him back and whispers the continuation of the story in his ear:

> And so the moon found a way to keep her love [...] an inn that once sat at one crossroads now rests at another somewhere deeper and darker where few will ever find it, by the shores of the Starless Sea [...] It is there, still [...] This is where the moon goes when she cannot be seen in the sky (308).

Their lips are not quite touching, but before Zachary can close the distance in a kiss, they hear a thunderous noise. The ground shakes and suddenly, they are in an empty room. The carved door has fallen from its hinges. Another tremor strikes, sending rocks over their heads.

Chapter 9 Summary: "a paper star splattered with gold paint"

The owls watch as the Starless Sea rises, and they fly over its waves. They screech, calling out warnings and celebrating that the long-awaited time has finally come. The Starless Sea floods the Harbor, reclaiming the Heart and all the books within the Archives. The end is here and the Owl King arrives, "bringing the future on his wings" (310).

Chapter 10 Summary:

Zachary Ezra Rawlins and Dorian fall back through the wardrobe as the tunnel collapses behind them. Zachary grabs his bag, and the two of them run for the Heart. Before they reach it, they hear shouting and Dorian pulls him back. He announces that he needs Zachary to know that what he feels for him is real. Stunned by both the confession and the timing, Zachary cannot form a reasonable response before Dorian continues walking.

When they arrive the Heart, the universe clock is broken, and the shouting grows louder. The Keeper's voice insists that he did not allow anything and that he understands. Allegra answers coldly, insisting that he does not, but she *does* because she has seen where "this" leads and will not permit it to occur. Seeing Zachary, she remarks that she knows someone who will be pleased that he is still alive. Zachary cannot tell who she is addressing, but she announces that someone (either him, Dorian, or both) does not know why he is there. She declares she has unfinished business with Dorian and draws a gun on him. The Keeper pulls her arm back, causing the bullet to ricochet instead of killing Dorian as planned.

A fissure opens up in the floor and Allegra slips, falling toward it. She grabs Dorian's coat and pulls him in after her. Zachary's eyes meet Dorian's as he and Allegra fall, and he remembers Dorian's last words to him: *"I don't want to lose this"* (314). Dorian is gone, and the Keeper is pulling Zachary away from the edge of the fissure as he screams.

Chapter 11 Summary: "a paper star that has been unfolded and refolded into a tiny unicorn but the unicorn remembers the time when it was a star and an earlier time when it was part of a book and sometimes the unicorn dreams of the time before it was a book when it was a tree and the time even longer before that when it was a different sort of star"

The son of the fortune teller walks through snow, carrying a sword whose sisters are long gone; one melted down and the other sunk into the ocean. The sword is now in a scabbard that was once used by an adventurer who died trying to protect someone she loved. The sword, her love, and the rest of her story were lost, though songs were sung about her at one point, however inaccurate. The son of the fortune teller looks toward a distant light, clothed in history and myth. He believes he is almost there but actually has far left to go.

Interlude IV Summary: "Another place, another time"

Twenty years before the present day, the painter packs up to leave after years of "watching and painting and trying to understand and now that she understands she can no longer simply watch and paint" (316). On her way out, she leaves a case of paints and brushes outside a door, instructing a cat to make sure that "she" gets it. This request is a decision the painter will later regret.

The painter takes the scenic route to the Heart. She has left a painting in her studio, which she is sure will be hung up by someone at some point. She does not know the subjects of the painting, but "they are there in the story of the place, for now" (317).

She looks up at the clockwork universe, seeing two different images through her different eyes: one it is as it is, perfect and complete; the other, burning and broken. She resolves to change this particular story. She passes the area where she had once rolled dice: all swords and crowns. In that moment, she sees "a golden crown in a crowded room" and "an old sword on a dark shore, wet with blood" (317). As she rides the elevator upward, her eyesight clouds and the images fade, to her relief and terror.

Of all the countless stories she has seen in that eye, she has never seen herself leave the Harbor. By doing so, she is breaking her vow, but she feels that if she can change this part of the story, she can change the fate of the place.

The painter steps through the door onto a beach. She kicks the wooden door until it breaks, then burns the remaining wood. She has an object in a jar in her bag that will be "insurance." If she closes the doors, she can stop the return of the book and everything that happens in her vision after that. She keeps the doorknob as a way to keep a piece of the Harbor with her, then sobs next to her fur coat. Then, she resumes the identity she had before becoming an acolyte: Allegra Cavallo.

Book 4 Analysis

The story continues toward narrative coalescence, maintaining its usual stylistic components. The smaller stories continue to connect to the larger narrative and to offer more information on the circumstances leading to the present conflict. Book 4, Chapter 1 tells the story of the stag who waits to be shot, one of the stories that Eleanor tore from *Sweet Sorrows* because she didn't like it. Chapter 3 describes a girl forced to eat paper containing stories of the person she's supposed to be. One key divergence is that, in Chapter 11, the story reflects events which have not yet transpired in Zachary's life: a reference to him walking through snow, carrying a sword. Chapter 9 also relates an ending for the Starless Sea—when the Owl King returns, and the sea rises up to reclaim the Heart and the Archives—but the book's meandering, circular timeline makes it unclear if this event happens in the future or in the past.

Book 4 reveals Allegra Cavallo as the painter of the bunny pirates as well as all the other paintings in the Harbor. She is not a guardian, as Zachary supposed earlier; she became an acolyte, but sacrificed an eye instead of her tongue. Allegra's lost eye opened her mind to visions of stories that happened or will happen, which she dutifully painted. When she saw two separate visions of the universe clock with her good eye and her missing one, she saw a bleak future for the Starless Sea and resolved to prevent it. She left behind her paints and one final painting, which Zachary will see later.

As she exited the Harbor, Allegra destroyed the door behind her. She kept the doorknob; ostensibly, it now hangs in the Collector's Club with all the others. She left paints and brushes behind, in the hopes that "she" would find them. She also took an object inside a jar, which she placed in her bag, calling it an insurance policy. Although the significance of these actions will be revealed later, it's clear that the doorknobs aren't merely trophies of the doors destroyed. They help Allegra maintain an emotional connection to the place she loves so much. She wants to preserve the Starless Sea from the fate she saw in the universe clock. She is the story's antagonist, but she operates from a sense of protectiveness, not with the intent to destroy.

After sharing a bottle of wine, Zachary and Dorian explore the wardrobe in Zachary's room. Dorian asks if Zachary has entered it in search of Narnia, a reference to C.S. Lewis's *The Lion, the Witch, and the Wardrobe.* Along with the reference to *A Wrinkle in Time* in Book 3, and the connection of Allegra to the Norse myth of Odin (a god who gave one eye so he could see all that happened in the world), the author connects the story in the Starless Sea to real-life existing stories in addition to the fairy tales she creates herself.

Within the wardrobe, Dorian and Zachary find a carved door that depicts a celebration and multiple phases of the moon. Behind the door, just as was depicted in the carving, they find a party. Dorian spins out the story of the lovelorn moon and the innkeeper from Book 2, Chapter 7, adding new material: The moon asked Time to move the innkeeper to a place out of time and away from the stars, so she could continue to visit her lover. In return, the moon agreed to figure out a way for Time to hold onto Fate. The story of Time and Fate has been mentioned in each book so far and is a key to the novel's resolution.

Before Dorian and Zachary can celebrate their requited affections, the Harbor suffers terrible earthquakes, and Dorian is plunged into the darkness below it after Allegra grabs at him to steady herself. Just like all the previous couples, Zachary and Dorian are now separated. Before their separation, they found Allegra with the Keeper, and the universe clock was broken. She declared that she had "unfinished business" with Dorian and tried to shoot him.

Foreshadowing continues to build with visions, ominous paintings, carved doors, and plot points: a crown in a crowded room; a sword on a shore wet with blood; the painting of the moonlit forest with keys and a man trapped inside it; a door carved with two figures in cages, one reaching for the other, in a city with a curved tower. A fire also consumes the dolluniverse room and "claims it for its own" (300). Later, this occurrence (and phrasing) will be repeated on a larger scale.

Book 5: "The Owl King"

Chapter 1 Summary

The Keeper drags Zachary Ezra Rawlins away from the fissure and into his office. The Keeper tells Zachary to breathe and gives him a drink that does not make things better as promised; it makes them clearer and sharper, which feels worse. Zachary glances at the Keeper's notebook and sees that it is full of passionate love letters—in poetry and prose—all focused on Mirabel. The Keeper strikes the doorframe, making it crack, then puts his hand back on the frame, which knits itself back together. The stones around them shift and the chasm fills back up. The Keeper announces that Mirabel was in the antechamber and that he will not be able to retrieve her corpse until the rubble is cleared, which will take time.

Zachary rolls a die, which lands on the heart as expected, then asks what the symbol means. The Keeper explains that the dice determine what fate awaits a new arrival. Hearts are for poets who "wore their hearts open and aflame" (325). Zachary asks whether more than the three paths mentioned in *Sweet Sorrows* exist. The Keeper answers that all have their own path, and that symbols offer an interpretation, not a determination.

Zachary observes that the Keeper has lost Mirabel before. The Keeper confirms, saying that he always loses her, whether to circumstance, Death, or his own stupidity; years later, she always returns. This time, however, Mirabel believed that something had changed, but she never explained why. Zachary remembers the story of Time and Fate as the Keeper continues: The person Zachary calls Max lives in vessel after vessel, sometimes remembering her past lives, but not always. The previous incarnation,

Sivía, died in a fire in the Harbor. The Keeper gathered what he could of her remains and placed them in the urn Zachary saw in the crypt beneath the Bee Queen statue. The Keeper thought that Sivía would be his love's last incarnation. Instead, she returned as Mirabel.

When Zachary asks how long the Keeper has been there, he answers that he always has, rolling the die on the desk but not checking how it lands. Zachary sees that it is a key as the Keeper takes him through his office, passing a jar with a hand in it—the one Mirabel took from the Collector's Club.

In the back room past the office, Zachary sees a shelf filled with notebooks, like the Keeper's notebook full of love letters to Mirabel. On the wall, there is a large painting of Zachary, bare-chested but wearing pajama pants, holding a sword in one hand and lifting a feather in another. Behind him, with one arm wrapped around him, Dorian whispers in his ear. One of Dorian's palm is covered in honeybees; the other hand is covered in chains with keys dangling at the ends of them. A golden crown is above them, and a starry sky beyond it. Zachary's open chest reveals his heart, painted in gold and covered in flames, glowing like a lantern and casting light over them. It is the last painting, the Keeper explains, that Allegra completed in the Harbor. The Keeper explains that he has looked at it for 20 years, so he knew Zachary and Dorian's faces, but did not know how long it would take for them to arrive.

Zachary remembers Mirabel's recounting of how she met Dorian—his attempt at murdering her—and remembers how she said that it didn't work. In light of that, something has indeed changed. He and the Keeper hear a sound at the doorway and turn to see Mirabel: "Change is what a story is, Ezra. I thought I already told you that" (329).

Chapter 2 Summary

Dorian continues falling, unsure of how long it has been; he has long since lost sight of Allegra. Something he thinks may be a planetary ring strikes his shoulder, breaking it. He sees a light below him and expects that he will soon crash into whatever the bottom is. He thinks about Zachary and all the regrets he has for the things he did not do. He remembers Mirabel and the night that changed everything for him, but doesn't regret it, despite how things have gone.

Rather than striking bottom, Dorian falls through a cavern toward the light. As Dorian gets closer and closer to the ground below, his final thought is "Maybe the Starless Sea isn't just a children's bedtime story" (331). Perhaps, there might be water below. He plunges into the Starless Sea and realizes that it is not water, but honey.

Chapter 3 Summary

Mirabel and the Keeper have a heartfelt reunion, complete with a raw, heartfelt embrace that makes Zachary uncomfortable. Mirabel states that there is a plan, which people have worked toward for centuries; the only problem is its execution. She announces that they are going to rescue "Ezra's boyfriend," retrieves the broadsword in the Keeper's office from its case, and knocks over a container of keys. The Keeper protests, but Mirabel points the sword at him and answers firmly, "I love you but I will not sit here and *wait* for this story to change. I am going to make it change" (333). She gives the sword to Zachary and leaves to change her clothes, leaving the Keeper to stare after her.

Zachary announces his realization that the Keeper is the pirate and Mirabel is the girl; "all of the stories are the same story" (334). The Keeper explains that it was long ago in an older Harbor and that word "pirate" would have been more accurately translated as "rogue." Back then, he was the Harbormaster until it was decided that the Harbor no longer needed a master. The Keeper was forced to watch as they executed Mirabel in his place by drowning her in the Starless Sea.

Zachary takes his bag and the sword and goes to the elevator. Mirabel says that Allegra attempted to close the door from the other side. She asks if Zachary loves this place. When he answers that he does, she tells him that Allegra loves it more. Mirabel explains that her mother disappeared when she was five and Allegra raised her before leaving when Mirabel was 14. Despite raising Mirabel for nine years, Allegra repeatedly tried to have her killed because she saw her as a danger to this place.

Mirabel says that they are in what Zachary's mother would call a "moment with meaning" (335), mentioning that she had met her. Zachary is startled but more concerned with the elevator, which sits below the floor and drops a bit when Mirabel steps inside. Noticing him hesitate, she reminds Zachary that he said he trusted her. He steps into the elevator. It plummets into darkness.

Chapter 4 Summary

Dorian struggles to stay afloat in the current of honey. Just as he thinks, "What a stupid, poetic way to die" (337), someone grabs his hand and pulls him up and over the edge of a boat. He is instructed to stay down as claws strike his shoulder. He is handed some cloth and wipes the honey off his face so he can open his eyes. A girl announces that the owls are gone but will return as they like knowing when things have changed. Dorian notices that while his shoulder is no longer broken, he now has a tattoo of a short sword with a curved blade, a scimitar, on his chest.

He sees Allegra's body laid out on the deck. The woman explains that she knew Allegra as "the painter" and mentions that she used to play with her paints when she was a rabbit. When her answer startles Dorian, she explains, "I used to be a rabbit. I'm not anymore. I don't need to be. It's never too late to change what you are, it took me a long time to figure that out" (340).

Dorian asks her name. She says that they called her Eleanor up there, though it is not her name. Confused, Dorian thinks she does not look old enough to be Mirabel's mother. He tells her that his name is Dorian, which feels truer than his other names. Inspecting Allegra's body, he sees not a tattoo of a sword on her chest, but a bee, which surprises him.

Eleanor informs Dorian that she can take him to the place tattooed on his back if that is his destination. The tattoo shows a cherry tree forest in bloom, with lanterns and lights all through the branches. At the center, an owl with a crown sits on a beehive that drips honey onto a stack of books atop a tree stump.

Chapter 5 Summary

Zachary Ezra Rawlins dreams of dancing in a ballroom only to be awoken by Mirabel. Having somehow survived the elevator crash, they are in a courtyard surrounded by stone arches. He notices one has a key and another has a crown. Mirabel explains that it is a lost Harbor, one abandoned as the Starless Sea rose, with another one appearing higher up. She lived three lifetimes in that

Harbor, which she remembers, along with all her other lifetimes.

Mirabel explains her mortal lives and their relation to the plan she had referenced earlier: "I was always going to be mortal until I was conceived outside of time. People who believed in the old myths tried to construct a place for that to happen. They attempted it in Harbor after Harbor" (345). People at the Keating Foundation worked to enable her birth, though most died before she could offer her gratitude. Mirabel muses that for all the time spent planning, they did not consider the consequences of their actions.

Zachary realizes that they are rescuing Dorian because Mirabel has seen the painting. He observes that they are not there to find Dorian, but to find Simon, the last thing lost in time. Mirabel corrects him: Zachary is there in order to do something that she cannot. When he asks whether he *had* to, Mirabel explains that fate does not take away from Zachary's agency and responsibility. A massive parliament of owls interrupts their argument, and Mirabel tells him to run.

In the darkness, Mirabel and Zachary are separated. Zachary swings the sword, wounding some of the owls, but he cannot escape them fully. He runs until he finds a staircase ending above his head. He tosses the sword on the lowest stair and tries to jump toward it. He grasps the sword but loses his grip and falls into the darkness below.

Chapter 6 Summary

Dorian asks Eleanor about his new sword tattoo. She explains that he *thought* that it should be there, so the sea listened. When he insists that it was only an idea, she explains: "It's a story you told yourself. The sea heard you telling it so now it's there. That's how it works" (351).

She explains that she found parts of the ship and told herself the story of it to build the rest of it. Dorian confirms that he had his back tattoo before falling into the sea. When he had lost *Fortunes and Fables*, all that remained was the photocopy of the illustration. He had wanted something no one could take away from him, something he could always keep close.

Eleanor takes Dorian into her cabin, where a stuffed bunny with an eyepatch and a sword sits on a shelf, alongside an antlered skull and feathers. She shows Dorian her map of the changing layout. When he asks how much of this realm is comprised by the sea, she explains that the sea is really more of a series of rivers and lakes. She gives him directions back to the Heart, but warns him that it will be different. Dorian explains that he is trying to get back to a person, instead of a place. Eleanor points out that people change, too. Dorian agrees but does not want to think about it.

Eleanor explains that time is different "down here," passing more slowly and sometimes "skipping around" rather than passing at all. Dorian asks if they are lost in time and Eleanor answers that he might be, but she is not. She came down searching for someone, then searched for and found herself. After that, she started exploring again, feeling as though it is what she should have been doing all along.

Allegra's body is tied to a wooden door. They set it out to sea and set it on fire using one of the lanterns. Eleanor mentions Allegra's belief the dead should be returned to the sea, since it is the source of stories and all endings are beginnings. She wonders if that means that "all beginnings are also endings" (355). Dorian can only answer, "maybe." After the funeral, Eleanor thanks Dorian for "seeing" her when other people "looked through [her] like a ghost" (356).

Chapter 7 Summary

After his fall, Zachary Ezra Rawlins has landed in a "sea of broken statues" (357). He takes a torch from one of them, lights it, and starts walking. The rubble beneath him makes for uneven ground, but he continues on. When the stones shift, he bumps into a corpse and takes its scabbard to make carrying the sword, which he still has, easier.

Zachary finds his way to a tunnel. As his torch dims, he suddenly hears sounds he is not making and comes face to face with a giant white rabbit. He hears a voice berating him for believing in any of it, saying he died friendless because he was too caught up with his books to make a real life for himself. All he sees is his mind's way of creating the life he wanted: full of adventure, intrigue, and even romance.

As he considers the rabbit's words, someone with a British accent grasps his arm and tells him not to listen. Zachary resists, and the voice in the darkness becomes angry, trying to grab him. Zachary focuses on his sword and the new person. He insists he still believes. As his determination grows, walking becomes easier, but the thing in the darkness follows.

The British voice tells Zachary to wait. Zachary sees a sliver of light from a door and then is pulled through it. The darkness fights back, hissing when he stabs at it with the sword, claiming that he does not know why he is there and that he is being used. The door closes. The man asks for

Zachary's help in barring the door. Zachary looks around and finds himself in a temple, staring at Simon Jonathan Keating.

Chapter 8 Summary

Dorian dreams of his failed attempt to kill Mirabel. He wakes on Eleanor's ship and puts on the clothes and boots she has found for him. The coat has stars for buttons. They reach the shore, and Dorian sees the forest of blooming cherry trees within the cavern. Eleanor tells Dorian to tell the innkeeper that she says hello. He agrees and mentions that he knows Eleanor's daughter; Eleanor knows he means Mirabel but says Mirabel is not her daughter "because she's not a person. She's something else dressed up like a person, the way the Keeper is" (367).

Dorian wants to give Eleanor something out of gratitude for saving his life. Realizing that he has *Fortunes and Fables*—and that what truly bothered him about not having it was that it was not being read—he offers it to her. Eleanor says that she once gave someone a book that was important to her and never got it back. As the boat leaves, he sees "to Seek & to Find" carved on its hull (368).

Dorian enters the forest, which is exactly as described and illustrated in his book. As he gets deeper into the forest, he sees stumps covered in books or melted wax from still-burning candles. He follows a clear path away from the sea; the falling cherry blossom petals turn to snowflakes. The path grows darker and colder until Dorian cannot see. He hears something moving around him and lights a match, revealing a man who has the head of an owl standing in front of him. The match goes out, leaving Dorian in darkness in front of the Owl King.

Chapter 9 Summary

Zachary Ezra Rawlins sits face to face with Simon Keating, whose left hand appears to have been cut off at the wrist. Simon asks if Zachary can still hear the voice from the darkness. Zachary says that he does not. Simon tells him that the voice told him lies and that Zachary should let it move through him and then let it go.

As Zachary calms, he notices the statues, some of which have animal heads. The statues have outstretched arms, crowns, and antlers, tied to balconies and doors with ropes, ribbons, and threads, which have book pages, keys, feathers, and bones attached to them. In the atrium, he sees a sequence of moons sculpted in brass. The two largest statues, with balconies built around them, face one another from opposite sides of the room; one figure is obviously the Keeper. Red ribbons wrap around his fingers and wrists, tying him to both balconies and doors, and to the statue that both does and does not resemble Mirabel. Mirabel's statue has red ribbons around her neck and wrists, which fall to the floor and pool like blood.

Simon asks "which one" Zachary is: the heart or the feather. He says it is confusing that Zachary carries the sword but does not wear the stars and that Zachary should be somewhere else. Zachary mentions the bunny. Simon calls it the celestial hare and says that seeing it means that the moon has arrived and it is later than Simon had thought. He notes that the Owl King is coming. When Zachary asks who the Owl King is. Simon answers, "Its wings beat in the spaces between choices and before decisions, heralding change [...] of the long-awaited sort" (373).

Zachary asks who the stars are, and Simon answers that *they* are the stars—they are all stardust and stories.

Flummoxed, Simon states that things are not right: The doors are closing, ending possibilities. Once within the story, Simon exited it and now monitors the story as the sea and the bees whisper it. He tries to understand the story's shape, its past, and its future. He tries to record it, but fails.

Zachary understands that the array of statues, ropes, gears, and keys is Simon's representation and record of the story. He notices paper bees surrounding a sword and crown, a ship run aground, a library, a city, a fire, a pit of dreams and bones, someone in a fur coat on a beach, a cloud (or possibly a blue car), and a cherry tree with blossoms made of book pages. As the ribbons and keys shift, images within the pages grow clearer: vines around the orange cat in the Keeper's office, two women drinking and talking at a picnic table at night, a boy standing in front of a painted door he does not open. When Zachary looks from another angle, the whole thing seems to be in the shape of an owl, but the shape dissipates into individual pages again. After the change, he notes that some people once together are now separated. It is snowing somewhere. Someone is walking toward an inn at a crossroads, and the moon has a door in it.

Simon observes that the story is changing again, with events moving so fast that they've begun to overlap. Time may move at different rates, but all progresses toward the future. His comments grow more cryptic: "She was holding it in like a breath and now she is gone. I did not think that would happen [...] soon the dragon will come to eat the world [...] The story followed you here. This is where they want you to be" (374). When Zachary asks who wants him to be there, Simon whispers that gods with lost myths are writing new ones.

A breeze ruffles the book pages and ribbons, putting out candles. Zachary backs into a statue. On the statue, an owl sits, staring at him. Zachary tries to draw his sword, but Simon asks, "Why would you fear that which guides you?" (375). He explains that the owls propel a story forward. This owl, small and fuzzy, drops a folded paper star at Zachary's feet and waits for him to open it. Zachary unfolds it and reads as the owl looks on.

Chapter 10 Summary: "The Door in the Moon"

"The son of the fortune teller stands before six doorways" (376).

Chapter 11 Summary

Zachary Ezra Rawlins only reads the first few words, not ready to know the rest of the story—his story. He folds the paper back and puts it in his pocket. He considers that all three of the things lost in time are with him—the book, the sword, the man. The instructions said "find man," but now that he has found him, Zachary is unsure of what to do next.

Simon mutters cryptic advice again: "You are words on paper. Be careful what stories you tell yourself" (378). When Zachary asks for clarification, Simon asks if he is new and states that he believed he was there "to read and not to be read, but the story has changed" (378). Simon tells Zachary that Zachary is inside the story, with Dorian and his sword, and a cat searches for him. Simon notes that he sees many symbols now, when once there was only the bee.

Zachary declares he must find Mirabel, but Simon insists that she is not his friend and that if she has left him, it was intentional. Simon again says that Zachary should not have brought the story there; he stays away from it because attempting to return only brought pain. His first attempt ended in fire. During his second attempt, Allegra cut off his hand. Simon says that Allegra is now gone, surprising Zachary, but then suggests that they leave before the sea rises.

Zachary asks if the representation of the story says that Zachary goes with Simon. Simon checks, but says he is unsure who Zachary is. Zachary answers that he is the son of the fortune teller, but Simon no longer recognizes his own name. Zachary understands that Simon is truly a man lost to time—he sees but does not remember. Hoping to remind Simon of his identity, Zachary gives him *The Ballad of Simon and Eleanor*.

Simon repeats his earlier statement—"we are words on paper"—but adds a foreboding new sentence: "We are coming to the end" (380). Zachary suggests that reading the book will help Simon remember. He opens and shuts it quickly, saying they do not have time. As Simon asks if Zachary will join him in his ascent, the owl grips Zachary's shoulder, but Zachary is uncertain what that means. Zachary looks at the story, then considers the people who have passed through the temple and felt what he feels: uncertainty, fear, and the inability to be sure of making the right choice. He asks Simon how to get to the Starless Sea.

Chapter 12 Summary

Dorian, cold and dark, stands in front of the Owl King and offers his hand. The Owl King takes it and silently guides him to the inn at the crossroads, which has a crescent moon doorknocker on a blue door. When the innkeeper settles Dorian in by the fire, he sees Dorian's star-shaped buttons and sword tattoo. Startled, the innkeeper announces that his wife left something for him, though she mentioned that he might not know he was looking for it. He gives Dorian an elaborate box, carved out of bone with gilded designs. On the top of the box, crossed keys are surrounded by stars. The sides have bees, swords, feathers, and one solitary crown. Dorian asks if the innkeeper's wife is the moon, but he laughs and says the moon is just a rock and his wife is his wife.

Dorian notices no seams and no obvious lid, but there is a six-sided impression on the bottom of the box in one of the full moons. He looks over the symbols and wonders what is missing. He sees bees, keys, a crown, feather, swords, owls, and cats; finally, he realizes there is no mouse. He asks the innkeeper if he has a mouse. The innkeeper laughs. He says that he had told his wife that he missed mice after his inn was relocated, so she brought him silver mice. One of his mice is fashioned as a knight with a tiny sword, and its base has six sides. Dorian presses it into the indentation of the moon and turns the mouse. The lid opens. Inside the box, he sees a human-like heart, beating.

Chapter 13 Summary

Zachary Ezra Rawlins follows Simon's directions to the sea. Eventually, he comes across a tent with food and other provisions. He finds Simon's old coat, which he puts on, leaving his sweater behind. He quickly realizes that he will not be able to fit all of the items in his bag and sees a note in the center of the table: "When you're ready/choose a door" (388).

Zachary returns to the path and finds six doors with the expected symbols on them, though they are out of order; the crown is at the end and the bee is in the center, next to the heart. He recognizes the situation as the one in the paper star that he refused to read further. He returns to the tent and enjoys the food and the brief reprieve from whatever is about to happen. The tent and its provisions remind him of the health potions in front of a door in a video game, which often hint at danger ahead.

Zachary drinks his wine and thinks about everything he has learned so far. He tosses the paper star into the fire, unread. He finds the doors again with their golden symbols; sick of doors, he continues past them, venturing into the shadows through crystal and ancient architecture. Eventually, he finds the outline of a door scratched into a crystalline cavern. This is another meaningful moment, possibly the most significant of them all. As he stands in front of a new door, Zachary Ezra Rawlins knows the right path: "The path that leads to the end" (391).

Interlude V Summary: "Another place, another time"

Two years after the present (according to Zachary's timeline), Kat Hawkins drives her sky-blue car to Madame Love Rawlins's farmhouse in the Hudson River Valley. Madame Rawlins gives her a warm welcome. When Kat asks if she is worried, Madame Rawlins answers that worrying will not change the future. Kat still worries about Zachary and the things they still cannot safely discuss.

She tells Madame Rollins a secret that she has not told anyone: She created a video game for her thesis, designed for Zachary. It began as a choose-your-own adventure story with smaller stories and myths within stories with multiple endings. She then turned it into a text game. The company that hired her wants her to create a full-blown version for them. Madame Rawlins observes that Kat thinks Zachary will never play it, and she assures Kat that he will want to play it when he comes back.

Madame Rollins says that she once had her cards read by a good reader. All that she told Madame Rawlins came true except one thing: She said Madame Rawlins would have two sons. At first, she assumed the reader was wrong but now, she knows that she was right, and that Zachary will come back because she has not yet met her son-in-law. The pure acceptance in the statement makes Kat smile, even though Kat is unsure that Zachary will return.

Kat unloads Zachary's belongings from her car, including the Ravenclaw scarf she knitted for him. She leaves him a keychain flash drive with "<3 k" written on it. She puts her teal notebook down next to it but changes her mind as she is not yet ready to part with it. Madame Love Rawlins gives Kat advice, ranging from the overarching to the mundane, and a message of love and acceptance.

Madame Rawlins invites Kat to Thanksgiving and tells her that though she thinks she has no home to go to, she does now. On her way back to her car, Kat decides that if Madame Rawlins is sure that Zachary is alive, then he must be.

Book 5 Analysis

Book 5 begins with Zachary mourning for Dorian, who unbeknownst to him has actually survived his fall. Pulled from the Starless Sea made of honey, Dorian finds himself on a ship captained by Eleanor, who is the bunny, Simon's lover, and Mirabel's biological mother. Dorian previously saw a ship on the Starless Sea, with books stacked on its deck, when he peered through a telescope in Book 4, Chapter 6.

Eleanor takes Dorian to the same location represented in the tattoo on his back, which he took from an illustration in *Fortunes and Fables*. The cherry tree, with its forest in bloom, is where Dorian meets the Owl King, previously mentioned in Book 4, Chapter 9 as a herald of the story's end. When Zachary is rescued by Simon and sees his statue-populated re-creation of the story, Simon refers to the Owl King as a "plot device" and says that owls move the story forward. Simon also says that if the celestial hare has arrived, then the moon has also arrived and the Owl King is near—all signs that the story of the Starless Sea is nearing its end. Simon asks Zachary to leave with him, before the sea swallows everything. Pieces of the universe clock sink into the Starless Sea, hinting at how the sea will eventually reclaim everything in the underground world.

Just as Allegra painted the images that appeared through her missing eye, gathering pieces of the story but never truly understanding it, Simon does his best to record the story. His cryptic symbols foretell future events: a sword and crown surrounded by a swarm of paper bees, a city, a library, a shape like a cloud or a small blue car, a cherry tree with book-page blossoms, among others. Yet he also cannot understand it—containing the entire story and understanding its significance is a keeper's task.

Simon has not only forgotten his place in his story, but who he is. His unique perspective is a foil to the story-telling test of the potential keepers. Having wandered out of his own story, he is not where he is meant to be, but lost in time and lost to himself. He has tried to reenter the story multiple times; the second time, Allegra cut off his hand— ostensibly, it's the hand she had in the jar as an "insurance policy," the hand which found its way to the Collector's Club.

Although certain omens, like the dice rolled in the Harbor, make predictions about a character's arc, the characters have free will and can make choices that change the story. Zachary has a history of blaming fate for his decisions and their outcomes. Mirabel accuses him of being paralyzed by fear, saying he is unwilling to act unless following instructions. Zachary finally takes control of his own storyline when he burns the paper star, a page of *Sweet Sorrows* that could tell him what happens next. By burning it without reading it, he reclaims his agency and chooses to make his own decisions, uninformed and unbiased. As the Keeper reminds Zachary, "Each of us has our own path, Mister Rawlins. Symbols are for interpretation, not definition" (325).

Time shifting isn't the only thing that makes reality within the Starless Sea realm hard to define. The characters seem to have the ability to write new elements of the story, thus forming reality from their thoughts and the stories they tell. Eleanor found the pieces of her ship; she told herself how it should be put together, and it came together. When a tattoo of a sword appears on Dorian's chest, Eleanor tells him that the Starless Sea heard him think that the sword should be there and created it. Dorian mentioned earlier that he had not taken any further tests to become a guardian, yet the guardian's sword is branded into his chest anyway after he explored the shores of the Starless Sea—as though he was fated to have it. Simon says that Zachary is words on a page, and that Zachary should be careful about the stories he tells himself; those stories could become the basis for the reality in which Zachary exists. Simon's statement makes a larger point about the nature of people and the reality they experience. Two people can experience the same set of circumstances and perceive them very differently; everyone's lived reality is constructed of the stories they tell themselves.

Many events in Book 5 set the conclusion of the story in motion. Mirabel knocks over a jar of keys, hinting at the fate of a person who is the "key" of the story, the one responsible for bringing the story to its end and locking it away. Zachary falls into a darkened pit after tossing his sword onto a stair and jumping to grasp it, setting in motion the events that will lead to his death. Dorian's cherry forest is within a cavern; Zachary also enters a cavern. Most importantly, the innkeeper's wife leaves a box for Dorian, which contains a beating heart. The box is the one sculpted by the story sculptor, and the innkeeper's wife is the moon, who, in the story Dorian told in Book 4, Chapter 8, promised Time that she would find a way to help Fate put itself back together. Dorian and Zachary will play a critical role in Fate's reincarnation, with significant consequences for Zachary in particular.

Finally, Zachary's friend, Kat, who taught the workshop that he helped to moderate, reappears in the interlude between Books 5 and 6. She drives a blue car—Simon's story representation showed either a cloud or a blue car—and has formed a relationship with Zachary's mother. Madame Rollins was once told that she would have two sons, and she feels confident that Zachary, who has been gone for two years in her timeline, will return with her future son-in-law. Kat will continue to appear in future chapters and has a future in the Starless Sea.

Book 6: "The Secret Diary of Katrina Hawkins"

Chapter 1 Summary: "excerpt from the Secret Diary of Katrina Hawkins"

Kat wrote in her journal because she no longer trusted the internet. She took all her notes off her laptop. "They" erased her phone and the notes on it, so she tried put in what she remembered of them. Although she questioned whether she would be able to read her handwriting later, she hoped that "wherever this all leads it's worth it" (401).

Without overt evidence of foul play, no one seemed interested in investigating Zachary's disappearance. When the police asked how well she knew him, she just said "friends." They asked if he might have done something, hinting at suicide, and she answered that she did not think so, but she also thought that most people were not too far away from that and life could unexpectedly shove a person in that direction. The police took her number but never called. She left messages, but they did not respond.

Chapter 2 Summary

Inside the cavern, Zachary Ezra Rawlins finds himself in the snow, standing in front of his mother's farmhouse during a holiday party. He sees a stag in the woods, but it quickly disappears. Zachary is confused when someone who looks like Dorian appears, asking about his lack of an ugly Christmas sweater. Zachary asks Dorian questions, but despite the reasonable answers, Zachary is certain it this is not the real Dorian.

Dorian claims that for the last year, Zachary has had difficulty separating fantasy from reality. Zachary insists that he does not have "episodes," but he is confused and it is hard to breathe. Dorian assures him that they will get through it, leaning in to kiss him in a habitual way, but Zachary insists "this is a story that I'm telling myself" (407). Dorian feels real as Zachary pushes him away. Zachary sees the moon in the sky and tells it and himself that they are not supposed to be there at that moment.

Zachary tells Dorian that he has to leave. He walks away from the house and wonders if it is a test. He walks back to the field, but the door is gone. He tries to remember the map he saw and did not take, but ultimately decides it does not matter: "If this is a story he is telling himself, he can tell himself to go forward" (408). He yells at the moon that they are not supposed to be there. The moon does not answer, but watches, waiting to see what will happen.

Chapter 3 Summary: "excerpt from the Secret Diary of Katrina Hawkins"

Kat convinced the IT department to check Zachary's emails when the police did not bother. The Collector's Club deleted any trace of emails between them in the month of January. She broke into his room and found an odd slip of paper under a sock under the bed; in the middle, she saw a drawing of a bee, a key, and a sword.

Frustrated by the confusing clues, Kat researched the charity that threw the ball—the Collector's Club—and discovered it was a subsidiary of another charity, which was a part of itself. She discovered an address and learned that the building burned down around the time of Zachary's disappearance. When Kat walked around the building, she noticed the iron gate had a sword at the center.

Kat registered on a dark net conspiracy theory site, posting, "Looking for info: Bee/Key/Sword" (413). She received a response from an admin, reading "don't." When she replied saying that it was not spam, just a question, the admin responded, "I know. Don't. You don't want to get into that" (413). She received another message from a new account: "Crown/Heart/Feather/The Owl King is coming" (413).

Chapter 4 Summary

No matter how far Zachary Ezra Rollins walks, the woods do not get any closer. He puts *Sweet Sorrows* in his coat pocket and abandons his bag of equipment, taking only the books. Zachary informs the moon, "If Dorian is down here somewhere I want to see him. Right now" (415). Suddenly, someone is running toward him. He draws the sword only to find it is Dorian, who assures him that it is really him. Zachary asks where the moon goes when she is not in the sky, but Dorian's smile reassures him that it is not a fantasy even before Dorian answers that she goes to the inn that was once at the crossroads. Dorian is both there and somewhere else at the same time.

Dorian says he thinks he may have fallen asleep in the inn as he does not remember leaving it. They embrace and Zachary realizes that he would be perfectly pleased to lose himself in Dorian. Dorian asks if Zachary is in the "world beneath the world beneath the world" (415). Zachary explains that he arrived in the elevator with Mirabel, and Dorian suggests he try to make it to the inn. Zachary acknowledges that they might not be in the same time anymore, but Dorian insists that they will find each other and figure it out together. Zachary gives the sword to Dorian, who suddenly vanishes. Zachary now stands alone in the snow, with no sword and no moon.

A stag, with golden antlers covered in candles, stares at Zachary. Their eyes meet, then the stag turns and walk toward the trees. Zachary follows it. They make it into the woods more quickly than expected, and Zachary notices that the bark on the trees is actually gold leaf. The stag guides him to a clearing. He looks up at the sky, noticing the moon is gone; when he looks back down, the stag is missing, too. The trees are covered in ribbons with keys strung on them.

In the center of the clearing, he sees a seated figure he thinks is Mirabel, but it is actually a carved figure made of ice. Her gown's fabric ripples are waves with ships, sailors, and sea monsters. The face is a precise likeness of Mirabel. A red light glows from within her chest, the ice making it look pink. Her hands hold a torn ribbon without a key. She gazes at an empty chair across from her. Zachary sits on it. He imagines her voice as she asks the pirate to tell her a story. Like the pirate, Zachary obliges her.

Chapter 5 Summary

Dorian wakes up, still feeling the snow and the sword, though he is in his warm bed at the inn with his blankets in his hand. He dresses and tells the innkeeper he needs to leave. He opens the door, but instead of the snowy forest, he sees a shadowy cavern. He thinks he can see a castle in the distance. The innkeeper tells him to close the door, saying that the inn "can only send you where you are meant to go, but that is a depth where only the owls dare to fly, waiting for their king. You cannot go there unprepared" (420). Dorian asks what he needs, but before the innkeeper answers, the door opens, revealing the moon. She walks straight to Dorian, gives him the sword, and asks if he is ready.

Dorian confirms where Zachary is and announces that he is going. While the innkeeper fetches his bag, the moon tells Dorian that the inn is a "tethered space" unaffected by the sea's tides. Once he leaves, he will be untethered and unable to trust anything he encounters. She explains that things in the shadows will use his own thoughts to frighten, confuse, or seduce him; because they are at the edges of story/myth, he may have difficulty navigating. She urges him to hold tight to his beliefs. When Dorian asks what happens if he doesn't know what he believes, the moon kisses his hand in answer.

The innkeeper returns his bag, heavier now with Fate's heart in it, and blesses him, giving him a light kiss. Dorian sets off, unable to understand the warnings the wind tries to give him.

Chapter 6 Summary: "excerpt from the Secret Diary of Katrina Hawkins"

Kat was not sure of where she heard of the Owl King. When she asked Elena what she talked to Zachary about after the class, she said the books were still missing, so Zachary might have them. Elena also gave Kat the name of the donor: J. S. Keating. Through research, Kat found Jocelyn Simone Keating, born in 1812, possibly disowned, with no marriage records or records of children. Her brother was married with no children, only a "ward" who was listed as dead as a teenager.

Kat was both confused by and interested in the prospect of a woman born in 1812 somehow leaving books to multiple universities in different countries, some of which had not existed before the woman must have died—and there was no record of her death. Elena helped Kat find the other donated books, and she realized that they were all too modern to belong to a woman from the 1800s. Elena could not find any information on the Keating Foundation but knew that one of the books had the bee, key, sword combination drawn on the back cover.

Kat received a text from an unknown number reading, "Stop snooping, Miss Hawkins" (423). She did not reply, but all texts to and from Zachary disappeared from her phone.

Chapter 7 Summary

Zachary is uncertain where to start, but the ice statue's request that he tell her a story has no specifics. He tells his own story, beginning with the painted door he did not open, his sense of not belonging anywhere, his fears that none of it matters, his bad relationships, the university library becoming his haven, finding *Sweet Sorrows*. He reads *Sweet Sorrows* to her, and recites stories from *Fortunes and Fables*. He tells her how he had always been searching for something and was disappointed that the Harbor did not make the feeling go away—but nearly kissing Dorian did. He tells her about crashing in the elevator, the voices in the darkness, finding Simon, the fake holiday party at his mother's house, the stag, and everything until he has run out of story. Then, he makes it up.

Zachary wonders about where one of the ships on her gown is going, watching it move as he does. Around it, the forest changes as the ship sails through the trees, making them fade. He continues the story about the ship as the snow melts around it. Zachary imagines himself, Dorian, his owl, and the Persian cat on the ship as it takes them to undiscovered lands. He sees an unopened door marked with a crown, a heart, and a feather. The door leads to "another Harbor on the Starless Sea, alive with books and boats and waves washing against stories of what was and what will be" (426). When he runs out of the story, he brings it back to the present moment. He stops and the ship returns to the gown.

Leaning in, Zachary whispers in her ear: "Where does it end, Max?" (426). Her head turns toward him, and she takes the key from around his neck that had once fallen out of the binding of *Fortunes and Fables*. She stands, pushes her palm and the key against Zachary's chest, then draws him in for a kiss. It is overwhelming and agonizing, but when he cannot take it anymore, he opens his eyes and she is gone, along with the forest and its keys. He has the image of the key burned into his skin.

Zachary now stands in an alley with a new ice figure of a boy staring at a wall with a painted door. In the center, Zachary sees a bee above a key above a sword. He touches the paint and turns to see the boy is gone. He grasps the doorknob, turns it, and steps through to the Starless Sea.

Chapter 8 Summary

Dorian is surprised by the behavior of the things in the dark. Even the moon's warnings did not prepare him for their vicious cruelty as "they use his own stories against him" (429). Fortunately, he is armed with a sharp sword and has skill in using it. He finds himself in different places, under attack, but he understands what is happening and refuses to allow the things in the darkness to win.

Chapter 9 Summary: "excerpt from the Secret Diary of Katrina Hawkins"

Kat knew they were watching her, even as she wrote in her notebook at the Noodle Bar. She noticed a man in line behind her drop something into her bag. He pretended to read while he watched her. His behavior reminded her of the man who watched Zachary at the bar. Eventually, the covert operative left, and Kat found a small, sticky transmitter stuck to the inside of her purse. She knew she would not have found it if she had not seen it planted.

When Kat returned home, she cried and admitted that she thought Zachary was dead: "I think at some point I stopped looking for *him* and started looking for *why* and now the why is messing with me" (433). She put the transmitter on a cat in the park.

Chapter 10 Summary

Zachary walks through a door and into a cavern, though he wonders whether he has actually been in the cavern the whole time. The Persian cat pushes against his ankle, nudging him toward the ridge ahead. Zachary finds himself standing on the shore of the Starless Sea. It glows in an amber tone. He breathes in, but instead of the expected scent of salt, the air is sweet. He walks to the edge and takes off his shoes. He runs a hand over the waves and licks it, finding it not salty but unexpectedly saccharine.

Zachary wonders what happens next but then dismisses the idea. For the moment, the Starless Sea is his whole world and nothing else matters. Looking up into the darkness, the structure above him looks vaguely like a castle. He thinks about how far he has come. Hearing footsteps, he expects the newcomer to be Mirabel, but he discovers that it is actually Dorian. They stare at each other and Zachary considers how he cannot breathe and maybe this actually is love—except he literally cannot breathe. He looks down toward his chest and sees Dorian's hand wrapped around a hilt of a sword just before all goes dark.

Chapter 11 Summary: "excerpt from the Secret Diary of Katrina Hawkins"

Kat sat at the Gryphon in a secluded booth. Allegra sat down across from her. Kat quickly identified the woman as the "big guns." After picking at Kat's missing friend and recent breakup, Allegra pitched her on the Collector's Club, claiming that it would give Kat an opportunity to belong. When Kat declined, Allegra attacked her academic career and future chances. Although tempted, Kat held firm. Something did not feel right about Allegra, who dodged Kat's questions about Zachary.

Kat asked whether Zachary worked for Allegra or burned her clubhouse down. Allegra responded that she can give Kat answers, but first Kat must agree to the terms. She asks if Kat was curious. Kat *was* curious, and she knew that if she said no, she would never see the mysterious woman again. She said no anyway.

Allegra asked if there was anything she could say to change Kat's mind. Kat asked what happened to her eye. Allegra told the truth, saying that she sacrificed it to be able to see "the whole story" (441), though it no longer worked. Kat looked into her eye, startled to see a stormy sky with lightning instead of the expected cataracts. Kat stood up, saluted, and left with her things. The business card lay abandoned on the table. Allegra said that she was disappointed and Kat knew what came next: "We'll be keeping an eye on you" (442).

Chapter 12 Summary

Zachary Ezra Rawlins is dead, surrounded by a quiet, empty darkness. Somewhere, a faraway voice greets him. Suddenly, he is in his body—or a version of it. He is still wearing his pajama pants without shoes and has his key brand, but no wound or heartbeat. His vision is perfect, despite his having no glasses.

Zachary is frustrated by death, realizing that he found what he was looking for in Dorian only to lose it. He considers that Dorian may not have known that it was really him, the way he did not know it was really Dorian in the snow. By giving Dorian the sword, Zachary set his own death in motion: "It feels as though all of the pieces were put in place to lead to this moment and he put half of them there himself" (444). He is angry with himself for the things he regrets doing, the things he regrets not doing, and the wasted time he will never have back. Most of all, he is angry at Fate. He remembers what Mirabel said about his purpose: "You're here because I need you to do something that I can't" (444). Mirabel always knew that he was going to die.

The sea in front of him is not the same Starless Sea: This one is made of confetti and streamers. The castle behind him is made of cardboard and the stars above it are folded paper. He sees an entire paper universe, including a city across the sea with a twinkling light emanating from it. Suddenly calm, Zachary spots a rowboat and picks up an oar. Dead or not, he understands what is next: "Apparently he isn't finished with his quest […] Fate isn't done with him, even in death" (446).

Chapter 13 Summary: "excerpt from the Secret Diary of Katrina Hawkins"

Kat decided to focus on work after meeting with Allegra. Someone left a brass, feather-shaped key in her campus mailbox. It had a tag reading, "For Kat when the Time comes" (447). She put it on her keychain. Despite Kat's expectations, Allegra never returned.

Kat worked on a new project and came up with a game-based format for storytelling. It was a genre-spanning, branching story with multiple options and plots, an attempt to incorporate the things possible in a game but not in a book.

Kat found Simone Keating through a friend in London. The Keating Foundation seemed to be an underground, unofficial library society "for people who were not allowed in the standard societies" (448). Since it was unofficial, there were no "proper" records, just notebook fragments and a few photographs.

The journal snippets mentioned catalogued doors, missed contacts, being between incarnations, spending time below, and J. moving papers to the cottage. Other fragments mentioned six doors, a place existing "outside of time," and a "final incarnation" (449). She saw a picture of a blonde woman labeled "Simone" and a blurry group photo. One of the names on the back of the group photo was "J. S. Keating," connected to a blonde woman who was clearly "Simone." A caption was written below the names: "meeting of the owls" (450).

Chapter 14 Summary

Zachary Ezra Rawlins rows across the paper sea toward a lighthouse made from a wine bottle. From farther away, the castle looks real, complete with a dragon's shadow around a tower. He finds the city and walks through it to a town, crossing a key bridge and a book-paper meadow. Some of the pieces of his surroundings are obviously repurposed objects, but others are exact miniatures.

Zachary realizes he is in the dolluniverse. He makes his way to the house that looks more real than everything else. Its lanterns are lit, waiting for him. There is a buzzing sound and the door opens. There is a sign above the door with the Rawlins family motto: "Know thyself and learn to suffer" (453). The buzzing increases until it forms words of greeting.

Chapter 15 Summary: "excerpt from the Secret Diary of Katrina Hawkins"

Over a year after Zachary disappeared, Kat had learned no more about Jocelyn Keating or the Owl King or the feather key. She had all of Zachary's belongings in her apartment and a history of "phone tag" with Madame Rawlins. A few months ago, she had seen a photograph from the masquerade party of a woman and a man. The man was Zachary, but when she tried to load a larger version and save the file, it was deleted.

Her thesis project took her to a meeting in Manhattan. While there, she received a text from an unknown number. It told her to go to the northeast corner of Union Square at 1 p.m. and was followed by emojis for a bee, a key, and a sword. The location was in a farmer's market; she looked up to see her knitting former student, Sarah, standing in the window of a bookstore. Kat remembered that they had had a conversation on overlapping narratives, "how no single story is ever the whole story" (456).

The pay phone next to Kat rang, and the text message to her phone prompted her to answer. On the line, Sarah admitted her name was not Sarah and confirmed that Kat turned down Allegra's offer. "Sarah" explained that she joined to belong to something but that the organization was dismantled and no one knew why. She said she contacted Kat to let her know that they were not watching her anymore.

Kat asked why Sarah did not look for the place they supposedly protected, and Sarah answered that her contract said they could kill her if she tried. She also said that they would kill her if they knew she was talking to Kat. Kat asked what happened to Zachary. Sarah answered that she did not know; she sounded panicked and looked over her shoulder. She said she knew that it was all over now. When Kat asked who the Owl King was, Sarah hung up and walked away. When Kat texted Sarah's number, the phone displayed a delivery failure. Kat did not know how to begin to search for a place that might not even exist.

Chapter 16 Summary

Zachary Ezra Rawlins stands in a doorway of a life-size dollhouse filled with a huge honeycomb and cat-sized bees. He asks why he is there, and the bees answer that it is because he is dead, so he is between places. They also say he is the key that she said she would send—the key to lock the story away when it was finished.

Zachary asks who told them that, not expecting them to answer that it was the "story sculptor." The bees explain that she is sometimes but not always in the story, that she is sometimes pieces and a person at other times. The bees are eager for Zachary's company and have awaited him for a long while. They thank him for bringing the story here as they "cannot lock away a Harbor story that has wandered so far away" (460). He asks how to get out, and they answer that there is no out, only in, nor is there a next because this is the end. The bees are concerned that he is not happy because he likes the story and the bees; he is their key and friend and he said he loves them. When he protests, the bees remind him that he did say so after they gave him cupcakes. Zachary realizes the bees are also the Kitchen.

In the library, he sees a brick dollhouse surrounded by a moat made of honey. The bees tell Zachary that it is the next story since "this one" is ending now and the key will "lock it up and fold it and put it away to be read or told or stay where it was tucked away" (461). The bees are not sure of what will happen after it ends, but they are glad to have company for the ending as they do not always have that luxury.

At the back of the house, he sees the cracked porcelain doll sitting in a chair looking out the window. Zachary announces that the story cannot end yet because Fate still owes him a dance. The bees offer to build a place where he could speak to the story sculptor or dance with her for a short time as they cannot talk to her themselves since she is not dead. The bees go to work building "the story of a space within this space" (463).

Chapter 17 Summary: "excerpt from the Secret Diary of Katrina Hawkins"

Kat remembered she heard of the Owl King at a party a few months before Zachary disappeared. A pink-haired woman offered her a drink and told her a fairy tale about a hidden sanctuary of a land that called out to people in their dreams, singing a siren song, and sometimes presenting them with a door. The land had a port on the Starless Sea.

Kat remembered that the hidden kingdom was a temporary space, meant to vanish because it had a beginning, a middle, and an end. It had been moving toward the end but it "got stuck," repeatedly starting over. Some parts of the story were trapped outside of the story space and other pieces got lost, but worse, "someone was trying to keep the story from ending. But the story wanted an ending. Endings are what give stories meaning" (466).

Although Kat was not certain if she believed that endings were the only things that give a story its meaning, she thought that a story needed to have some kind of place for the reader, player, or viewer to leave it—"a goodbye." Kat also believed that the best stories were the ones that felt as though they would always continue. She wondered if the story were a metaphor for learning to let go of things, or if other people would ascribe a different meaning to it.

In the pink-haired woman's story, the secret story space not only sang to people who needed sanctuary but also called for someone who would destroy it: "The space found its own loopholes and worked its own spells, so it could have an ending" (466). Kat remembered asking if it worked. Mirabel, the pink-haired woman, answered that it had not yet, but someday would. Kat also remembered a sad knight, something with a broken heart, a "Persephone-esque lady" who was perpetually leaving and returning, and a bird king whom she could swear was an owl. She did not remember what it meant in the story.

Chapter 18 Summary

The bees escort Zachary Ezra Rawlins to the newly made ballroom so that he may dance with Fate. He finds Mirabel waiting in a fairytale Max costume, this time with pink hair instead of a wig. As they dance, Zachary accuses her of making all of it happen, but she answers that she only gave opportunities: "I gave you doors. You chose whether or not you opened them. I don't write the story, I only nudge it in different directions" (469). He says it's because she is the story sculptor, but she answers that she is only a girl who is looking for a key.

Mirabel recalls one of her many deaths, this one drowning in the Starless Sea. While she drowned, she saw everything: all the harbors, the stars, the dance, and the end, but she did not know how they would get to it. She asserts that he asked for her because she could not really be there since she is not dead. When Zachary asks whether or not she is able to do anything and everything, Mirabel answers that she is a vessel—an immortal one this time, unsure of what, precisely, she is and what she can do.

Mirabel thanks Zachary for finding Simon and putting him back on his path. She laments that for all the conspiring to make her birth possible, no one considered her parents. Zachary observes that Allegra wanted to keep the book and cut off Simon's hand to prevent the story from ending. Mirabel agrees, explaining that Allegra did not want anything to change, but things became complicated:

> The story kept fading and the bees wandered back down to where they started. They followed the story for a very long time through Harbor after Harbor but if things don't change the bees stop paying as much attention. The story had to end closer to the sea in order to find the bees again. I had to trust that someday someone would follow the story all the way down. That there could be one story to tie all of the others together (470).

Zachary asks what happens next, and Mirabel answers that she doesn't know. She planned to get to this moment, but not for after. Zachary considers that nothing exists in this moment except for Max and that this moment matters, possibly more than all the others. Honey seeps up through the floors as the walls shake. Mirabel thanks Zachary, who again asks what happens now. Mirabel answers that it is not up to her; she provides doors, but others have to open them. She draws a door to a starlit forest. The rising flood of honey does not go through the door. She gives him an end-of-dance bow and he returns the gesture. When he looks up, she kisses his cheek and then leaves through the door.

The bees tell Zachary that it is time to go. He asks "where," but the buzzing has stopped. He goes up the stairs into the dollhouse, but both the bees and the porcelain doll are gone. The front door is sealed with wax. He climbs up the stairs and out of the attic onto the ceiling. Zachary watches from the widow's walk as honey bubbles up from under the confetti sea. The bees swarm above him, telling him goodbye, thanking him for being the key, and wishing him luck in the future. Zachary asks what future they're talking about, but they fly away into the darkness. The sea rises. He dives for the boat and falls into the honey. This Starless Sea pulls Zachary under and keeps him: "He gasps for a breath his lungs do not require and around him the world breaks. Open. Like an egg" (473).

Chapter 19 Summary

Rhyme is prepared for the end. She knows this story's every word and twist. She walks up to the Archives, noting the two empty spaces, and considers two missing books out of thousands to be an adequate performance. She still hears both the low hum of the past stories that have already been recorded and a small buzzing of the next few minutes, but there is no loud, demanding high-pitched future story as this place has no stories left. All of them are being reclaimed by the Starless Sea. She hopes that whoever recorded the last moments of the end has done a good job, and she knows from the sound that they have been recorded. She leaves the door to the Archive open for the sea, which follows Rhyme up the stairs to the Heart.

The Keeper has cut his hair, throwing his braids into the fire, complete with the pearls he had tied in for each year spent in this place. He continues to write to Mirabel in his notebook. Rhyme wonders whether he knows that Mirabel hears the whispers of what he writes. Before he closes his notebook, he writes, "This is not where our story ends. This is only where it changes" (476).

They move the painting of Zachary and Dorian, exposing a door. The Keeper asks where they should go and reminds Rhyme that the vows no longer matter. She says she would like to be there if they can. He looks at his watch, adjusting the hands, and nods, saying that they have time. The Keeper puts his hand on the door. He raises a glass, saluting the rising sea: "to Seeking." They go through the door. The sea takes everything returning all stories to their source. The Keeper and Rhyme walk along the sidewalk in a city with tall buildings. On a street sign at the corner of Bay and King, an owl perches and stares at Rhyme. "For the first time in a long time, Rhyme doesn't know what it means. Or what will happen next" (478).

Chapter 20 Summary

Dorian sits, staring at Zachary's corpse, numb from sobbing. He thinks about the first forms of the darkness that looked like Zachary. Believing it was him for only a moment was almost enough for the monster to kill him. Dorian did not hesitate to kill the following Zacharies, assuring himself that he would be able to tell when he saw the real person. He replays the moment of realization over and over in his mind. Now, there is nothing but grief, pain, and a Persian cat. He wonders if the pain will ever end and thinks he deserves it. He watches as the sea rises and resigns himself to drowning in honey. Then, he sees the ship.

Chapter 21 Summary: "excerpt from the Secret Diary of Katrina Hawkins"

Kat considered giving the notebook to Madame Rawlins but decided not to. She told her some of the information but not all of it. Madame Rawlins also just *knew* things. She placed a tarot card in Kat's pocket, which Kat noticed only later—the Moon. Kat looked it up and learned that it is "about illusions and finding your way through the unknown and secret otherworld and creative madness" (482). She put the card on her dashboard, so it stayed in view when she drove.

Kat tried to let go of everything, but she sensed something building, leading her to something new and next. Kat recognized that if things had not happened the way they did, she would not have started building her text game, gotten a new job, and launched a move to Canada. She felt as if she were following a string left for her by Zachary through a maze he might not even be in. She hoped he got his Ravenclaw scarf and that one day they would have dinner at his mom's place, with his husband, and that the good stories would keep them up late—"that the stories and the wine go on and on and on and on and on. Someday" (482).

Book 6 Analysis

Book 6 introduces Kat's point of view through excerpts from her diary. Unlike previous books, no new fairy tales stories alternate with Zachary's linear narrative. Though written in past tense, Kat's narrative takes place after Zachary's stories have concluded; for example, she finds the Collector's Club (destroyed by Mirabel when she and Zachary made their escape) already burned down. Two years behind her, Zachary continues toward his fate, assisted by what he understands from reading the other fairy tales. The presence of the moon, which he knows should not be visible because it is at the inn, lets him know that the Dorian he speaks to isn't the real Dorian. Later, when Zachary dies and finds himself in the in-between, he sees bees and a city; Simon's cloud/blue car is actually the blue car driven by Kat. The conclusion to his story (and the beginning of the Starless Sea's next story, as the Afterward will show) were foretold in the symbols in Simon's re-creation.

In Chapter 7, Zachary takes his final test for his role as keeper, as explained in Book 1, Chapter 13. He reaches a room filled with keys and is asked to tell a story to an ice statue of Mirabel. Like all keepers, he has chosen a story not his own and studied it for a year: *Sweet Sorrows*. He has learned it so intimately that he can tell the story as though he lived it himself: He can "relate the story as intimately as if [he] lived it [himself] as objectively as if [he] had played every role within" (76).

When Zachary is asked to tell the ice Mirabel a story, however, he doesn't exactly recount *Sweet Sorrows,* although he does read the book to her as part of the telling. He tells his own story and recounts his experiences in the Starless Sea; when he runs out of story to tell, he makes one up. As he spins a tale about one of the ships on her gown, the physical setting changes around him. In the chapters after his death, in the dolluniverse, he repeatedly asked Mirabel what happens next. What happens next, as will be seen in the Afterward, is the story Zachary makes up for the ice Mirabel.

After the test, a keeper is allowed to look around the room and choose a key with which to be branded. Zachary doesn't choose any of the keys in the space;

instead, he chooses the key that fell from *Fortunes and Fables,* the book he stole from the Collector's Club for Dorian. After branding, the new keeper sees every door, every key, and everything kept within. The former Keeper leaves with Rhyme and sets off toward a new life in an above-ground city.

As Zachary's test played out, Allegra tried to make the story end permanently by destroying all doors to the Starless Sea. Each closed door was a closed possibility, so Mirabel tried to reconnect the disparate pieces of the story by bringing together three lost things: a book (*Sweet Sorrows*), a sword (displayed in the Keeper's office), and a man lost in time (Simon). Mirabel told Kat that stories want and need endings; as such, she engineered a way for the errant pieces to be returned, so their storylines could be resolved and the greater narrative could end. Her solution is Zachary, the key, who finds the items lost in time and dies on the shore of the Starless Sea, gaining the attention of the bees and initiating the end.

As demonstrated by the library and implied by Kat's stories, however, the overall ending is only the beginning of a new story. The bees themselves confirm it, stating that there is no "next" within the story, but somehow Zachary has future endeavors ahead of him. In Zachary's timeline, Allegra failed to keep the story from playing out: Just as Simon predicts, and as the presence of the Owl King suggests, the story's end has come. The Starless Sea rises to consume all within its realm. It also sweeps into the Archive and reclaims the books that Rhyme leaves behind. Zachary falls in and prepares to die—again. As Allegra once stated, those who die on the shore are returned to the Starless Sea because the Starless Sea is the source of all stories.

Zachary's confusion over the tension between fate and free will continues. He realizes that his actions have led to his own death in accordance with Mirabel's plans to end the story, but she continues to insist that he has a choice. He comes to understand even more incarnations of Mirabel: She is the ice statue to whom he tells his story, the story sculptor who created the box for Fate's heart, and Fate itself. Zachary has received what he claimed all gamers wanted back in the workshop from Book 1: the ability to make choices within a larger narrative. For Mirabel—ironic because she is revealed to be the personification of Fate—choice is something to celebrate. She tells Zachary that she knew the overall plot of the story and its ending but not how they would arrive there.

Unlike the novelists who wrote the many books mentioned in *The Starless Sea*, Kat developed a game-based method of storytelling. Within this genre, certain constraints of the story already exist—fate—but the player's choices affect the outcome: free will. Kat told Mirabel that she viewed stories as needing an ending insofar as the player needs an exit, but she said the best stories feel as though they continue for all time in "story space." The Starless Sea is such a space, where stories continue for all time—where people who enter through its doors find exactly what they're looking for, and few ever wish to leave.

Although Zachary died on the shore of the Starless Sea, he continues to live in the in-between, and the bees say he has things yet to do. Stories, like Fate, have a way of pulling themselves together. The moon's promise to Time will be kept in the end.

Afterward: "Something New and Something Next"

Chapter 1 Summary: "Once, not so long ago…"

Dorian and the woman who was once a bunny but whose name is not Eleanor sail on the rising sea with Zachary's corpse bleeding on her maps. He hears a commotion on deck as the owls try to land on the sails to stay afloat. Dorian asks how high the sea will rise, but Eleanor assures him that there are many caverns and she knows how to navigate them all. Eleanor asks, and Dorian confirms that the body is his "person." She recognizes the coat he wears and asks what he is reading. Dorian shows her *Sweet Sorrows*. She is surprised to learn of its travels and smiles to have it returned, though it was never truly hers.

Eleanor tells Dorian that there is a man sitting on a precipice reading. She plans to pick him up when the sea level reaches it. Though she does not realize it, her words show that the person is Simon, the one she had initially been searching for: "I don't know how he'd get out otherwise, he only has one hand" (486).

Dorian hears Fate's heart beating and asks himself what the difference is between Fate's heart and a heart that belongs to Fate, kept in her care until required. Dorian looks back and forth between Zachary and the box, considering what he believes. As he opens the box, the heart beats faster: Its moment has finally arrived.

Chapter 2 Summary: "excerpt from the Secret Diary of Katrina Hawkins"

Kat found a note on her car that said "come and see" (488), with an address for a nearby vacant building. After some time, she decided to go in and discovered that it used to be a library. She saw paintings everywhere, with an unusual style: "like graffiti and Renaissance oil paintings had mural babies" (489). One of the paintings was of Zachary and Dorian, whom Kat recognized from the bar. Another of them was Kat in the clothes she was currently wearing with the notebook that was currently in her hand. On a particularly large wall, she a massive owl with a crown above its head. Under the Owl King, she saw a door with a crown, a heart, and a feather arranged in a vertical line down the center. Kat knew that the other side of the door was only a wall, but she had a key. She took her Moon tarot card and left her notebook in the car in case she did not come back.

Kat wrote to a future reader, saying that she was here and that these things happened, that it "might sound weird, but sometimes life is like that. Sometimes life gets weird. You can try to ignore it or you can see here it takes you. You open a door. What happens next? I'm going to find out (491).

Chapter 3 Summary: "…Fate fell in love with Time"

Zachary Ezra Rawlins wakes up with a new heart beating hard in his chest. He is alive and on a ship. He falls while trying to stand, but Dorian catches him. They stare at each other, then they laugh and finally kiss without the complications of distance, time, or fate.

Chapter 4 Summary: "Not the single story she requested but many stories"

Outside the former library, the Keeper flips through Kat's notebook and Rhyme looks through a window. Neither of them notices the approaching woman wearing a crown, but the stars do. She watches the Keeper read, then looks up at the stars. She holds a card out toward the moon. On the first side, the card shows a void—the ending—but on the other side, a bright expansion—the beginning. She turns it one more time, and the card dissolves into golden dust. She bows, straightens her crown, and walks to the car. She asks if the Keeper has been waiting long as he puts his jacket over her shivering shoulders. "Not long," he answers, though he has waited a long time for this moment.

Mirabel asks if Kat has opened the door yet. The Keeper says that she has not yet, but that she will since she has already shown her decision by leaving her notebook. He asks after Zachary. Mirabel says he is doing better: "He didn't think I'd let him have a happy ending. I'm kind of offended" (494). The Keeper suggests that he may not have thought he deserved one. Mirabel asks if that is what the Keeper thought. She reminds him that he does not have to be there now. He answers that neither does she, yet they are both there. She smiles; he tucks her hair behind her ear and pulls her in for a kiss. The new story begins: "Inside the brick building a door opens into a new Harbor upon the Starless Sea. Far above the stars are watching, delighted" (494).

Afterward Analysis

Mirabel and Kat's professed opinions on story endings both prove valid. The end does give meaning to the story, but the ending is also a "goodbye" where the reader can believe it continues in "story space." In that vein, the Afterward shows the story continuing in story space as the beginning of a new story. After Dorian places Fate's heart in Zachary's chest—foreshadowed in Allegra's painting of Zachary and Dorian, which depicted Zachary with a golden heart—Zachary and Dorian finally have their kiss and, according to the narration, their story is only beginning, as "no story ever truly ends as long as it is told" (492).

In this new story, each pair of separated lovers has been or is about to be reunited. Eleanor and Simon soon will be reunited on her ship. The inn at the crossroads, untethered in time, will also continue, allowing the moon and her husband their reunions. Even Time (the Keeper of the universe clock) and Fate (Mirabel) are reunited, beginning a new story. They choose to return to the Starless Sea, though they are no longer bound to it.

While Zachary's story has officially ended, a new one has begun—a concept epitomized by Mirabel's card, with ending on one side and beginning on the other. The card dissolves into the same golden dust as the egg, which symbolizes the story. The sky-blue car seen by Zachary in Simon's representation of the story is Kat's car sitting outside the library (also seen in Simon's representation); the library is where the new story will begin when Kat enters through a door into a new Harbor.

The story that Zachary told the ice-Mirabel echoes the new beginning, complete with a journey on a ship and a door to a new Harbor on the Starless Sea, this time marked with a crown, a heart, and a feather. As ending fades into beginning, the stars—which may include the reader— continue watching the latest story, "delighted." Zachary made his choices, but in the end, he received the happy ending foreordained by Fate.

CHARACTER ANALYSIS

Zachary Ezra Rawlins

The son of a fortune teller, Zachary is more inclined to believe in stories and magic than the average video games student. As much as he loves video games, he studies them more out of expectation fulfillment than passion; whether in a game or in a novel, his true love is the story.

His worldview is challenged when he discovers a book detailing an event in his life, when he had the opportunity to reach for a new world and failed to do so. Zachary embarks on a quest to discover all he can about the mysterious book, which leads him to a place and to Dorian, a person he did not know he was seeking. During his adventures, Zachary is forced to confront the concept of fate and his own tendency to lean upon it to absolve him of responsibility for his choices. Zachary's experiences challenge his ideas and empower him to take full ownership of his agency, creating the long-lasting bonds of relationship, which he has lacked and for which he has subconsciously longed.

Mirabel

Pink-haired and outspoken, Mirabel is never predictable. She insists on calling Zachary by his middle name and he returns the favor by calling her Max in reference to the costume she wore when they met at a literary masquerade. Born in the Harbor at the Starless Sea—the immortal daughter of Simon and Eleanor, conceived outside of time—she has the talent of painting doors that lead to her home.

Mirabel is an agent of change who draws Zachary and Dorian to the Harbor. She challenges Zachary's preconceptions and flaws, and fights for her own happy ending. As the newly immortal vessel of Fate, Mirabel guides the story to its end, so that she can resolve the remaining plot holes and permanently reunite with her lover, Time.

Dorian

The man who calls himself Dorian was once a member of the Collector's Club until one of his many assassination missions failed due to his target's immortality. Failing to kill Mirabel turned his world upside down, causing him to question everything. He did horrible things in the name of the protection of a magical world he has never been to, and now wonders whether he had any right to do so.

Dorian's misadventures lead him the Harbor on the Starless Sea and to Zachary. Despite his guilt over his previous dealings and his belief in his own unworthiness, he finds himself falling for the younger man and living out a story beyond his own imaginings in a place beyond his wildest dreams.

The Keeper

The Keeper appears to be an older man with braided hair, perpetually writing in a notebook. He is tasked with the keeping of the Harbor on the Starless Sea and always has been, forced to remain in the Heart of the Harbor for as long as it exists. Immortal yet powerless, he awaits his freedom, which is brought about by the story's end. His unflappable affect is belied by hidden depths of emotion, revealed by his own tragic love story. As the manifestation of Time, he continues to wait for Fate to return to him.

When Fate does arrive, their love is doomed by her mortality, which forces them apart once more. He is caught in the cycle of waiting and losing his love until the story can finally end.

Allegra Cavallo

Initially introduced as the "polar-bear woman" due to her white hair and white fur coat, Allegra is the leader of the Collector's Club, a secret society hell-bent on removing access to the Starless Sea by destroying all doors—and, if necessary, those who would open them.

Allegra's unexpected path to villainy comes from a place of love for the Starless Sea, where she lived as a child. She gave one of her eyes to become an acolyte and painted scenes from the stories taking place around her. She has a determination to never see the Starless Sea change, or for the story to wind its way to its end. Her deadly crusade literally shakes the temple of stories as she tries to stop Fate from guiding it to its conclusion.

Eleanor

A child-explorer who considers herself a bunny, Eleanor grows up in the Harbor at the Starless Sea. Her love of stories lead to far-reaching consequences when she lends her favorite book to her unexpected love, Simon. The book is then dislodged from the timestream and storyline, complicating the story's ability to end. Her trans-century love story results in the birth of the first immortal vessel of Fate: Mirabel.

Simon Keating

An unloved ward of his uncle, Simon longs for love and acceptance. He finds more than he expected of both when he finds his way to the Starless Sea—and when he falls in love with Eleanor, a bunny-eared woman from the future. His determination to reunite with her takes him beyond the limits of his own story.

Simon's unsanctioned decisions cause him to lose himself in time and eventually come to record and understand the larger story as much as possible. Although he fails to truly comprehend the events and the characters, his superior grasp of its meaning, including his observation that the owls move the story along and they should be trusted, guides Zachary to make the decisions necessary to lead the story to its conclusion.

Katrina Hawkins

Kat is a video game student in the same program as Zachary. The two are friendly, though she believes they are on the edge of becoming life-long, ride-or-die friends when he goes missing. Her tenacity prompts her to investigate the disappearance of her friend, drawing her into friendship with Zachary's mother, a conspiracy, and, eventually, a new world of stories.

Fate and Free Will

The Starless Sea explores whether a story's outcome, and its twists and turns, are fated by the story's structure or determined by the free will of those in the story. Zachary's preconceptions about the nature of fate are challenged both by his experiences and by Fate herself.

An Emerging Media student, Zachary acknowledges early on that gamers want the comfort of knowing that they exist within a greater narrative, but he does not accept that real-life humans want this same assurance in the external world. When he finds *Sweet Sorrows* and sees his own story, as the son of a fortune teller who bypassed a door to the Starless Sea, he wants to uncover the storyline laid out for him. He wants to have confidence in his actions because he knows his fate, and he wants someone else to blame should there be consequences. Mirabel—who, ironically, is the personification of fate—confronts this viewpoint directly: "You want to think that you did or that you were *supposed* to but you always had a choice [...] You don't do anything until someone or something else says you can" (346).

Zachary ultimately chooses to take the elevator into the Harbor because he, like all who enter the Starless Sea, is seeking. When they share a bottle of wine, Dorian toasts "to Seeking," and Zachary toasts "to Finding." To seek requires free will, but finding is never guaranteed; some may argue that fate plays a role in whether anything is found. Ultimately, Zachary learns to make his own decisions, discarding the page of the story that tells him what he does next and taking ownership of his own actions. Yet his freely chosen actions lead to his death, in accordance with Fate's plan.

Although Zachary operates within the same guidelines he had idealized as a gamer—making choices within an established plan—he is displeased when that framework leads to his death just when his life—and his love for Dorian—is beginning. Fortunately, Fate (ironically, the person who argued most for Zachary to embrace free will) creates a happy ending for him. Once he has served his purpose, her heart is used to bring Zachary back from the dead and give him a beginning to his new story with Dorian.

The Nature of Reality

Meta-storytelling elements, such as the characters reading stories about themselves, blur the lines between reality and fantasy throughout *The Starless Sea*. Characters learn, through their stories, about a larger narrative of which they are a part, although they never completely know how the story will end.

The nonlinear nature of time within the Starless Sea makes reality difficult to pinpoint. The Keeper describes time as a stream with many inlets: People can enter and exit at any point, and characters like Simon and Eleanor unite even though they live hundreds of years apart. Zachary finds that *Sweet Sorrows* contains the story of his encounter with a door, even though the book was donated to the library four years before the story took place. In another timeline, when Eleanor tore pages from *Sweet Sorrows*, Zachary discovered pages missing in his present-day copy. External events changed the story within the realm of the Starless Sea: the Keating Foundation interfered to have Mirabel conceived outside of time. Characters can also speak new story into existence; when Eleanor found broken pieces of a ship, she put it together by simply speaking about how it should be done.

If it's difficult to understand which events are real, it's even more challenging to determine what they mean. Zachary and Kat debate the nature of meaning early on during a class on Innovative Storytelling. The proposal is made that the meaning of a story is both personal and variable, determined by the one experiencing the story, and what has meaning to one person may not have meaning to another. Mirabel tells Zachary that the Starless Sea will disappoint him because it will never measure up to what he imagined in his mind. She says *Sweet Sorrows* is an interpretation of reality, not a description of it.

When reality and meaning are impossible to determine objectively, characters anchor themselves in people and in relationships. As Zachary tells ice Mirabel when he recounts his story, his life felt empty and without meaning until he met Dorian. The meaning of reality—the very nature of reality—may be as subjective as a story written by someone else. As such, "Not all stories speak to all listeners, but all listeners can find a story that does, somewhere, sometime. In one form or another" (187).

Endings and Beginnings

Endings are usually considered finite and concrete, disallowing any new action. In *The Starless Sea*, however, events that appear to be endings only pivot into a new line of story, both in each character's individual story and in the overall story. Mirabel and The Keeper's story is repeated again and again, with each taking on different physical forms throughout. The Starless Sea absorbs the realm above it when Zachary brings the current story to its end, only to begin again when Kat finds a new Harbor to enter.

When it becomes clear that the story within the Starless Sea is seeking its own end, the characters find themselves in an existential crisis, left to wonder what will happen next. They wonder whether their lives will continue if the story ends, what will matter if the story is over, and whether there will be any existence for them at all. Their understanding of stories make them think that endings are permanent, but even when Zachary dies, his life doesn't end—nor does it end the second time, when the Starless Sea absorbs the in-between.

Mirabel once told Kat that endings are what give stories their meaning; Allegra once told Eleanor that all endings are truly beginnings. In the Afterward, Mirabel gives the moon a demonstration of a magic trick: There is a card with void and ending on one side and expansion and beginning on the other. She shows both sides before the card dissolves into gold dust, just like the egg representing the story in the potential guardian trials. Just like the many lifetimes of Mirabel, the end is not the end, it is only a change; and after all, stories *are* change. "The world is strange and endings are not truly endings no matter how the stars might wish it so" (73).

Bees

Bees symbolize story; they are the things kept in the Starless Sea. This symbolism is present in the bee keys to the archive, the bee disks burned into acolyte's chests, the honey of the Starless Sea, and in the bees themselves, who appear to create the worlds for the stories.

Keys

The key is the symbol of the keepers of the stories, as burned into their chests. Unsurprisingly, the Keeper's roll of the die will always be the key—except for Zachary, who rolls hearts, foreshadowing the heart becoming the keeper's symbol in the new Harbor. The story must be locked at the end, and in this incarnation, the key is Zachary, though he also embodies other symbols at various times.

Swords

The sword is the symbol of the guardians, tattooed onto their chests. A particular sword also appears in several of the stories. It is first used to kill the Owl King; then, it sits in the Keeper's office. Eventually, Dorian uses it to kill Zachary, which brings the story to its end.

Crowns

The crown is one of the many symbols associated with the Starless Sea. It often appears above an owl, denoting the Owl King. It is also used on the outside of the new door to the new Harbor of the Starless Sea in the new story which has been created, along with the heart and the feather, taking the place of the bee in its imagery. Mirabel wears a crown and her father's dice roll is all crowns, suggesting that the crown is also a symbol of Fate.

Hearts

The heart represents poets and storytellers who share their emotions. The heart also appears in the story of Time and Fate, when Fate's heart is stolen by the mouse during her death (the ice sculpture of Mirabel, who is Fate personified, has a pulsing red light where her heart is missing). Fate's heart is later used to reanimate Zachary.

The central area of the Harbor at the Starless Sea where the Keeper resides is also known as "the Heart." The heart symbol replaces the key symbol in the imagery of the new Harbor. Zachary's dice roll is all hearts, indicating his nature as a storyteller.

Feathers

The feather is the final symbol in the series referring to the Starless Sea. It is on the key given to Kat to open the door to the new Harbor. The feather replaces the sword in the original sequence.

The Egg

The egg first appears in the initiation process for potential guardians. The guardian must protect an egg for six months before they are forced to crush it. The egg dissolves into gold dust, marking the guardian's hand forever. Allegra says that stories are like eggs: self-contained and fragile. Because people who love the stories want to live in them, their attempts to get inside the egg will break it. Simon describes the story's ending in this metaphor: "The egg is cracking. Has cracked. Will crack" (374).

The imagery is repeated when Zachary drowns in the honey after his death. In all these cases, the cracked egg is a symbol for possibilities and change beyond what is possible within the egg. This change can result in beautiful but permanent effects: "If an egg breaks it becomes more than it was and what is an egg, if not something waiting to be broken?" (245).

The Stars

The stars, when personified, are responsible for the murder of Fate. They appear in later stories as a commodity: something remarkable to be sold to the average in order to give their life a sense of greatness. Eventually, Zachary asks Simon who the stars are. Simon answers in a matter of fact tone, "We are the stars. We are all stardust and stories" (373), implying that humans are the stars—possibly including the reader.

1. "(The pirate is a metaphor but also still a person.)"
   (Book 1, Chapter 1, Page 3)

   *This aside points out the duality of being both a
   metaphor and a character. The pirate later proves to be
   the Keeper, who is also Time, making this an apt
   description. This duality also holds true for several
   other characters and ideas within the story.*

2. "Far beneath the surface of the earth upon the shores of
   the Starless Sea, there is a labyrinthine collection of
   tunnels and rooms filled with stories. Stories written in
   books and sealed in jars and painted on walls. Odes
   inscribed onto skin and pressed into rose petals. Tales
   laid in tiles upon the floors, bits of plot worn away by
   passing feet. Legends carved in crystal and hung from
   chandeliers. Stories catalogued and cared for and
   revered. Old stories preserved while new stories spring
   up around them." (Book 1, Chapter 2, Page 6)

   *This first description of the Starless Sea sets the tone
   for the ultimate setting and confirms the novel's
   magical realism. The Starless Sea is a place where
   stories are kept and where they originate.*

3. "And so the son of the fortune teller does not find his
   way to the Starless Sea. Not yet." (Book 1, Chapter 3,
   Page 13)

   *This last sentence in the third story describes the end of
   a significant moment in Zachary Ezra Rawlins's life.
   When Zachary reads this sentence, it puts the rest of the*

plot in motion, prompting him to investigate Sweet Sorrows *and ultimately find his way to the Starless Sea.*

4. "Anyone who enters the room affects it. Leaves an impression upon it even if it is unintentional." (Book 1, Chapter 4, Page 25)

    Although this description concerns the room with the dollhouse, it is also a larger metaphor for both the Harbor of the Starless Sea and for life. Even the smallest actions can have large and unforeseen consequences.

5. "Isn't that what anyone wants, though? To be able to make your own choices and decisions but to have it be part of a story? You want that narrative there to trust in, even if you want to maintain your own free will." (Book 1, Chapter 5, Page 35)

    In the Innovative Storytelling workshop, a student suggests that not only gamers want a collaborative story experience. She suggests that human beings desire comfort and the feeling that their steps are ordained, even when exerting their own agency.

6. "Everyone *is* a part of a story, what they want is to be part of something worth recording. It's that fear of mortality, 'I Was Here and I Mattered' mind-set." (Book 1, Chapter 5, Page 36)

    This moment not only speaks to the fact that each of the characters is in their own story (or stories) but also applies on a larger scale to humanity. People don't want to be forgotten; they want to be part of a story that matters.

7. "These doors will sing. Silent siren songs for those who seek what lies behind them. For those who feel homesick for a place they've never been to. Those who seek even if they do not know what (or where) it is that they are seeking. Those who seek will find. Their doors have been waiting for them. But what happens next will vary." (Book 1, Chapter 11, Page 62)

    The doors to the Starless Sea attract story lovers who are searching for a place to belong. This siren song is not only the premise of the book but also a hook for readers who may experience similar feelings.

8. "A quest has been set in front of him and he is going to see it through." (Book 1, Chapter 13, Page 87)

    Despite his growing fear for his own safety and decreasing confidence in his ability to separate reality from fantasy, Zachary decides to continue in his obsessive quest to understand his book and find the Starless Sea. It is his nature to answer the call of adventure, even if it is against his best interests.

9. "Occasionally, Fate pull itself together again and Time is always waiting." (Book 2, Chapter 1, Page 115)

    When Fate is murdered, Chance begins to dictate the outcomes of events in Time—but Fate finds a way to reconstitute herself. The tension between fate and free will is one of the book's major themes.

10. "No, each one's different. They have similar elements, though. All stories do, no matter what form they take. Something was, and then something changed. Change is what a story is, after all." (Book 2, Chapter 6, Page 153)

Mirabel argues that all stories are based in change and share that element, even if nothing else is similar. This perspective holds true over the course of the many narratives making up this novel.

11. "A story is like an egg, a universe contained in its chosen medium. The spark of something new and different but fully formed and fragile. In need of protection. You want to protect it, too, but there's more to it than that. You want to be inside it, I can see it in your eyes. I used to seek out people like you, I am practiced at spotting the desire for it. You want to be in the story, not observing it from the outside. You want to be under its shell. The only way to do that is to break it. But if it breaks, it is gone." (Book 2, Chapter 8, Page 175)

Allegra argues that no matter how much a reader may long to be a part of a story, attempting to enter it will only destroy it. She only sees one side of the story, however; when an egg breaks, it also unleashes something new.

12. "The old doors were crumbling long before Allegra and company started tearing them down and displaying doorknobs like hunting trophies. Places change. People change." (Book 3, Chapter 8, Page 248)

Mirabel states that things change even without the concentrated efforts of an antagonist. This reflects the fact that the story was already moving toward an ending and that Allegra's efforts to stop the Harbor from changing were futile from the beginning.

13. "A book is an interpretation [...] You want a place to be like what it was in the book but it's not a place in a

book it's just words. The place in our imagination is where you want to go and that place is imaginary. This is real [...] You could write endless pages but the words will never be the place. Besides, that's what it was. Not what it is." (Book 3, Chapter 8, Page 248)

Mirabel tells Zachary that he will not get what he wants from the Starless Sea because it will never be exactly how he imagined it, and it is his imaginary version which he longs for, rather than the reality. His imaginings were based on a book written long ago, and many changes have happened since then.

14. "Maybe this time will be different." (Book 3, Chapter 10, Page 260)

Mirabel tries to soothe the Keeper's worries that he will lose her again. She expresses the hope that things have changed enough for this iteration of the story to end differently.

15. "I think people came here for the same reason we came here [...] in search of something. Even if we didn't know what it was. Something more. Something to wonder at. Someplace to belong. We're here to wander through other people's stories, searching for our own. To seeking." (Book 3, Chapter 6, Page 297)

Dorian suggests that everyone who reaches the Starless Sea is responding to the same human longing for the extraordinary and a sense of belonging. He also suggests that they seek understanding of themselves and their own stories through the exploration of the stories of others.

16. "Each of us has our own path, Mister Rawlins. Symbols are for interpretation, not definition." (Book 5, Chapter 1, Page 325)

   After discussing the rolling of the dice, Zachary asks the Keeper if, unlike what Sweet Sorrows *had suggested, there are more than three paths. The Keeper answers that everyone has their own path and that the symbols are meant to help guide interpretation or nudge stories in one direction or another, but that they do not define who anyone is in a concrete way.*

17. "I love you but I will not sit here and *wait* for this story to change. I am going to make it change." (Book 5, Chapter 1, Page 333)

   Though the Keeper is concerned for her safety, Mirabel is determined to take control over her own narrative for the first time. This decision ultimately proves to be successful, leading them all to the end of the story.

18. "Important things hurt sometimes." (Book 5, Chapter 6, Page 352)

   Eleanor makes this observation after confirming that the tattoo of the illustration from Fortunes and Fables *was painful for Dorian. This seemingly innocuous statement is particularly poignant as it relates to the pervasive theme of lost love, which Eleanor, separated from her lover Simon, who is lost in time, knows all too well.*

19. "He had always wanted to be in the place but he didn't understand until he was finally there that the place was merely a way to get to the person and now he has lost them both." (Book 5, Chapter 6, Page 354)

Everyone who goes to the Starless Sea finds something they are seeking. Dorian realizes that, as much as he had longed for the literary haven, that which he had been seeking was Zachary. Now, he has lost Zachary, and without him, the place doesn't hold the meaning Dorian imagined it would.

20. "Why would you fear that which guides you?" (Book 5, Chapter 9, Page 375)

    Simon's statement about Zachary's fear of the owls confronts Zachary's assumptions about the elements of the story. The owls are a plot device designed to move the story forward, so Simon suggests that Zachary has no need to fear them, only to heed their guidance. Taking this advice empowers Zachary to find his way to the end of the story.

21. "A man this far into a story has his path to follow. There were many paths, once, in a time that is past, lost many miles and pages ago. Now there is only one path for Zachary Ezra Rawlins to choose. The path that leads to the end." (Book 5, Chapter 13, Page 391)

    For all that his choices have been his own, the climax of a story leaves few choices. Zachary has made it to the point in the story where the only way forward is to the end. He decides to take it.

22. "Whatever happens will happen whether I worry about it or not. It will happen whether you worry about it or not, too." (Book 5, Interlude V, Page 394)

    Madame Love Rawlins tells Kat that worrying solves nothing and that she should not waste her time with it. Although she speaks of Zachary's disappearance,

Madame Rawlins's advice also applies to real life, where people have no more control over certain elements of their narratives than the characters do in this story.

23. "Someone was trying to keep the story from ending. But the story wanted an ending. Endings are what give stories meaning." (Book 6, Chapter 17, Page 466)

    This moment shows the plot twist: The story itself wants to end, and all conflict to date has resulted from its unnatural longevity, brought on by Allegra's interference. This statement confronts the assumption that endings are negative and undesirable.

24. "This is where we leave them, in a long-awaited kiss upon the Starless Sea, tangled in salvation and desire and obsolete cartography. But this is not where their story ends. Their story is only just beginning. And no story ever truly ends as long as it is told." (Afterward, Chapter 3, Page 492)

    Repeating the phrasing used in the story of the pirate and the girl, this excerpt reinforces the underlying theme that endings are not bad, but necessary, and that they are inherently beginnings, too. It also offers the reader some comfort in the idea that there is no true end as long as a story is told.

25. "Inside the brick building a door opens into a new Harbor upon the Starless Sea. Far above the stars are watching, delighted." (Afterward, Chapter 4, Page 494)

    The last sentences of the novel show the promised new beginning found in the ending of the last story. They also show that the stars, who have long since regretted the murder of Fate, are pleased to watch this new story unfold.

ESSAY TOPICS

1. Morgenstern says that people enter the Starless Sea—the realm of story—because they want something they're not experiencing in the world above. Why do you read stories? What makes a good story, the kind that you never want to put down?

2. Morgenstern uses elements within other stories to foreshadow events in Zachary's story. Give some examples of foreshadowing throughout *The Starless Sea*. What do you believe was the most powerful element of foreshadowing in this book, and why?

3. Consider the Innovative Storytelling discussion, in which it's stated that people want to have agency within a larger, predetermined narrative. Do you agree? How do you think fate and free will play out in the course of life?

4. Think of a time when you've read or experienced a story and seen it one way, while someone else has had a completely different experience. How does a story get its meaning? How does the reader/player/viewer's experience affect the way they interpret a story, whether that story is textual or visual?

5. Mirabel says that once people have read a story, the real setting often disappoints because it doesn't match what they've imagined. Describe a time when you've experienced this disappointment—when you've imagined a setting and then been disappointed by the reality. What about a time when a real-life setting exceeded your expectations?

6. Mirabel posits that the nature of a story is change. How did the characters from *The Starless Sea* change as the story progressed? Why did Allegra want to prevent change within that setting?

7. The Keeper says that the symbols on the Harbor dice nudge the story in a certain direction, but they don't predetermine its outcome. What do you think the dice would show if you rolled them, and why? Do you like what you think the dice would say about you? If not, what would you change?

8. Give an example of a critical turning point for one of the characters, when they made a decision that affected the story's outcome. What would have happened if the character had made a different choice? How does someone make the right decision in a significant moment when they are not aware that it is a significant moment?

9. Characters in *The Starless Sea* often struggle to know what is real in a fantastic world, where timelines intersect and run out of sync. In your own life, how do you know that your perception of reality is true? What is the meaning of "real"? Can you describe a time when you thought something was real but were proven wrong?

10. Eleanor states that it is never too late to change who you are. Do you agree? Why or why not?